A Look

and othe...

PADRAIC FALLON was born in Athenry, Co. Galway in 1905. He moved to Dublin while he was in his teens, and his first poems were published there by 'Æ' (George Russell). He married in 1930, and had six sons, of whom four survive. His middle years were spent in Wexford, and it was there that he wrote a series of radio plays. He moved back to Dublin in 1963, and then to Cornwall in 1967, before returning to Ireland. His last years were spent in Kinsale, Co. Cork. Padraic Fallon died in 1974. His *Collected Poems* were published by Dolmen Press a few months before his death. In 1990 Carcanet published a new *Collected Poems* adding previously unpublished work.

BRIAN FALLON is the second of Padraic Fallon's six sons. He was born in 1933 and educated at St Peter's College, Wexford and Trinity College, Dublin. He was art critic of the *Irish Times* from 1963 to 1998 and its literary editor from 1977 to 1988. He is the author of six books, including *An Age of Innocence* (1998), a study of Irish culture from 1930 to 1960.

EAVAN BOLAND was born in Dublin and studied in Ireland, London and New York. She has received numerous awards for her poetry. She is director of the Creative Writing Program at Stanford University.

PADRAIC FALLON

'A Look in the Mirror' and other poems

Edited by BRIAN FALLON

With an introduction by EAVAN BOLAND

CARCANET

First published in Great Britain in 2003 by
Carcanet Press Limited
Alliance House
Cross Street
Manchester M2 7AQ

A CIP catalogue record for this book is available from the British Library
ISBN 1 85754 642 3

The publisher acknowledges financial assistance from Arts Council England

Typeset in Monotype Garamond by XL Publishing Services, Tiverton
Printed and bound in England by SRP Ltd, Exeter

this conjunction of rhythm and ethos x

a realising, honest music

captures to illuminate so x'

Contents

Introduction

At first glance, the poems in this book are fresh, quirky, even wayward. They are full of low stone walls, gulls and quays, the heather-grey distances of the west of Ireland and the grit of people abraded by landscape. They are talky and musical, both at once. They read like stories and sound like lyrics. But these surfaces are deceptive. In fact, these poems bring together disparate, even conflicting strands of Irish poetry. That tension, in the best sense, characterises Padraic Fallon's work. He was a local poet with a rare classical lexicon, a writer who sought out mythos and yet resisted the ethos he inherited, a stubborn laureate of the Ireland he found, unafraid of its violence and in love with the contradictions of its past.

It is also worth remembering that he was the inheritor of a difficult poetic moment and – in terms of his own identity – a flawed poetic bequest. Some of the poems in this book draw their vitality from just that. As he struggled with his inheritance, national and poetic, he remade the Irish poem. Indeed, the frame he created for Irish poetry – lyric, unprovincial and often unabashedly heroic – may be among the most interesting contexts made by any Irish poet in his century. But to see that context now, we need to look back at what it was then.

Padraic Fallon was born in Athenry in the west of Ireland. All around him were the echoes and whispers of a lost language and a broken past. Raftery haunts his poems, as much as the blighted fields and banished vowels. In historic terms, this was an eighteenth-century country. But as far as poetry went – and this was crucial – it was also post-Revival Ireland. In that sense, the Irish poets of the post-Yeats period – Kavanagh and Clarke as well as Fallon – had a task which would have daunted any writer. They were not merely chilled by the shadow of a great poet who had written them into subordinate positions in his poems. They also inherited, and had to contend with, an actual poem. The poem Yeats handed on was powerful in principle but of little use in practice. It had been useful, certainly, to Yeats who knew how to make the Irish cadence, and the Agonistes stance, disrupt the English tradition. But for these poets it was of little use. In their terms, Yeats had handed on a poem stranded somewhere between British Victorianism and Irish invention. It was the poem of an ethos which Samuel Beckett called, in a phrase of wonderful precision, *The Victorian Gael*. If like Yeats you were the foreground of that poem – in angry, eloquent and heroic close-up – then what was in the background hardly mattered. But if like Fallon, Clarke and Kavanagh you were lost figures in the unfocused background, where the faint shapes of beasts and trees and people happened in a simplified history, then the aesthetic of the Irish poem was compounded by an onerous ethic: how to tell the truth about a new people and a new poetry.

I think it's important to remember even today that poets such as Padraic Fallon had to take the Irish poem – used with brilliance by a great poet but inhospitable to their dignity, their identity, their Irish past – and re-work it. They had to write a whole psychic terrain into it; an act made more difficult in that Yeats had blurred that terrain with the power and enticement of simplification. Somehow, they had to resist those simplifications and restore that complexity. It was a task fraught with problems and contradictions.

The poems in this book make a rich but not always predictable progress through these contradictions. On the one hand, here is the locale of a rural, almost nineteenth-century Ireland, faithfully rendered and often luminously realised. Here is 'the low blue knoll/over the bog'. Here are 'the black miles' and 'the diminishing herds'. The sensibility that announces them is adamant and unsentimental: the enclosure and limitation are unadorned.

This is the moment to look more closely. The black miles, and all that low blueness are the habitat of historical claustrophobia and cultural darkness, to be sure. And if that's what these poems described they would be in a clear line of descent from Mangan – a dark psalm of lost opportunities. But Padraic Fallon is a deeply original poet, and in his way, a truly subversive one. This is not just the landscape of tragedy. It is also – and this is a salute to those eighteenth-century forbears – the locale of irony. In this, Padraic Fallon makes a sharp break with both the nineteenth-century Irish poets and Yeats's Irish pastoral. His Ireland is a distinctive, strange place, its shadows cast by Parnassus as well as the Twelve Pins. The landscape of these poems is one that is sometimes hard for humans to bear. But despite that, or even because of it, it is one that the gods might be expected to visit. And here – in this conjunction of mythos and ethos – the poems in this book show their wonderful spirit of irony and engagement.

To understand Padraic Fallon's vision, to see what Yeats called 'the fiery shorthand' of this quick-witted and tender-hearted poet, the best place to start in this book is the poem 'For Paddy Mac'. No piece here is more central to his powerful, disruptive view of Ireland and poetry. Here it all is. The dream of an Ireland that could be historic, even Homeric. The dream of his own post-Yeatsian generation, hungry to confirm the dignity of defeat through the destiny of language. This was the Ireland of the 1930s and 1940s – a hard enough place for a young poet to come to maturity in. One that was full of wishful thinking and beautiful delusion:

> Once, so long ago
> You used to probe me gently for the lost
> Country, sensing somehow in my airs
> The vivid, long-lipped peasantry of
> Last century
>
> And those bronze men
> With their diminishing herds far out on
> The last ledge of original earth,
> Fomorian types
> In the big one-eyed sky

And then the sharp coming down to earth: the earth of a people who were hard-pressed even to dream, let alone realise those dreams:

> That was my country, beast, sky, and anger:
> For music a mad piper in the mud;
> No poets I knew of; or they mouthed each other's words;
> Such low powered gods
> They died, as they were born, in byres.

This is Padraic Fallon's Ireland – a magnetic field of hardship, of loss, but also of possible recuperation through a scalding, honest music. 'For Paddy Mac' is an important, an essential Irish poem. It marks an argument which is too rarely heard: about place and displacement, about the hijacking of reality by wishful thinking.

I was fortunate enough to know Padraic Fallon. When I was young he seemed to me a figure both unexpected and exemplary. He possessed a blunt, truth-telling sensibility together with a contrary and tender-hearted lyric perspective. His originality, both of phrase and perspective, remains in my mind, and can be found again here in these poems. He was one of the poets who survived the rhetoric of the Irish Revival while keeping some of its aims and all of its energy. But he was more than that. There is something skewed and remarkable here if you look carefully for it: an Irish poem seen through the lens of an abandoned history and a recovered language. There are poets who make sense in their poems. And then there are poets who also make sense of the literature they belong to, and continue to shed light on it whenever their work is read. Padraic Fallon belongs to this second category. His poems continue to illuminate us.

Eavan Boland
Dublin, 2003

Writing on the Wall

Throw something to the gulls, any old scrap
As you go down the quays when day awakes!
Throw something to the gulls, they are so quiet, so keen,
In those soft moments when the dawn breaks
With a soft feathery explosion.

Anything, a bit of unblessed bread, throw it
To the gulls, throw something to the gulls.
Though they seem dropped bright feathers of dawn, a poet
Knows better. They are no eddying snowflakes
But bellies, appetites.

Throw something then, a pennyweight of bread!
Before one preying beak can gather it between
Wind and water, thousands are round your head,
A tumult, a squawking crown, wind-blown;
You are caught in a storm.

Cast your bread upon those waters, it will return
In a foam of birds that scrawls upon the air
A luminous word that will leave you insecure
Wondering how belly-hunger with this quill of rain and storm
Could forge such a dazzling signature.

Yeats's Tower at Ballylee

Is every modern nation like the Tower
'Half-dead at the top?'

W.B. Yeats

A pilgrimage is one slow foot
After the other, the agony of the heart
That looks to a place that will ripen like a fruit.
Yet I arrive in a Ford car
At the Tower talking of markets and wool
And corn drowned in the stook, the country around
Rain-rotten, the wet road buzzing like a spool
And trees at their year's end
Dropping the loaded sky to the ground.
I arrive talking of heifers and wool
And am confronted by the soul
Of a man in whom man cried like a great wound.

Somewhere a man will touch his image and burn
Like a candle before it. What happened here
In this ruined place of water and drowned corn
May still be here.
The oaken door hangs open, I go in
To a desolate underground that drips;
Shadows are on the stairs, the walls are weeping
A peacock paint, where a shoe slips
I clamber into a chamber like a tomb
Or a dim woodcut by William Morris
And suddenly I know the tower is
A boy's dream and the background of his rhyme.

Here where country blood was spilt
Neither earth nor stone cries out, for this is a dream-structure;
All that the brazen Norman built
To house a score of bullies in black armour
Deflected and turned to phantasy
By the boy who brooded on book and paint
Long mornings in his father's study
As medieval as a saint:
This is the Tower at last, its passion spent
And wearied of its own brutality
Where a boy could dream like Gabriel Rossetti.
Useless as verse and as magnificent.

I turn from the arty chimneypiece where glass
Has the pale wash of dreamy things and climb
Through a rude and navel arch, I pass
A sentry-go where no man turned a rhyme;
And the narrow stairway leads me to the place
Where he worked at the great table
Or lifted his tall height to pace
The enormous floor of his own fable;
Did he wear iron then, I wonder,
Or when the shadows stole the candle-light
Imagine himself all constellated night?
Il Penseroso in the magic chamber?

Yet nothing is here but the wind in the swinging windows
And the roar of the flood waters far below,
Not a house in sight, the corn in rows
Drowned and the drizzle rotting in the meadows:
The earth that cares for nothing but its seasons
Of lust and fruiting and death
Worked all about him here and gave no reasons
Why any man should waste his breath
In delicate definitions of a mild
World where man is the whole,
The individual soul
A heavenly cradle for the newborn child.

From the boy's dream to this reality
Of brutal weather and brutal stone
The Norman brought him. I come on the right day
To see for myself how earth can change a scene.
Rain and desolation, isolation
And fear in civil war can bring a man
To that harsh point in contemplation
Where soul no longer sees the sun:
In that bleak vision can man live,
Not summing up heaven and earth in measure?
Can he spend himself like a rich treasure
Where only the animal qualities survive?

Here at last he knew what opposites
War in one person. He became a man.
And the man divided into the primitive cross
Of two men in one rhythm. When the Norman
Came to the top the poet's words were blood
And what was good but a mere vision
Of arrogant foray, rape, and ride.
And then soul took its turn and with precision
Divined like an architect a house of life
Where violence had an energetic place
Only to find a holy face
Stare back serenely from the end of strife.

I climb to the wasting storey at the top.
His symbol's there where water and watery air
Soak through the plaster. The higher we clamber up
Into ourselves the greater seems the danger;
For the wider the vision then
On a desolate and more desolate world
Where the inspirations of men
Are taken by man and hurled
From shape into evil shape;
With the good and the grace gone out of them
Where indeed is there hope for men?
So every civilization tires at the top.

Around me now from this great height
Is a vision I did not seek. I have avoided it
And now I am forty-five
And wars blow up again, the east is lit,
Towns burn, villages are bombed,
With people everywhere in flight,
Their households on a handcart, or entombed
In homes that fell about them in the night
And dragging children homeless in the air;
A mass migration of the humble
Before some war-mad general.
O the higher we climb up the wider our despair.

This tower where the poet thought to play
Out some old romance to the end caught up
The dream and the dreamer in its brutal way
And the dream died here upon the crumbling top.
I know the terror of his vision now:
A poet dies in every poem, even
As blossom dies when fruit comes on the bough,
And world is endless time in which things happen
In endless repetition, every man
Repetitive as a pattern, no soul
But the sprawling spirit of the whole
Massing upon the careless earth like frogspawn.

Everywhere is the world. And not less here
Because the stream, dividing, moats the place.
To live a fairy tale he bought this tower
And married a woman with a pleasant face;
And built in bookshelves, cupboards, hung
His pictures up and walked around
His beehive and his acre, wrung
Some civilization from the ground:
And yet instead of rhyming country ease
As in the eighteenth century we find
Him raving like a man gone blind
At the bloody vision that usurped his eyes.

Below me in the road two countrymen
Are talking of cattle and the price of wool,
Glad of the gossip and something held in common.
That scene would have been peaceful
An hour ago, but now I stumble down
In horror, knowing that there is no way
Of protest left to poet or to clown
That will enlarge his future by one day.
I could beat a policeman, bawl in a square, do gaol
For something silly. And what avails it? I
Step into the drizzle of the sky
Despairingly, to talk of the price of wool.

Maris Stella

1

In the flat glaze of the quays,
On wet stone where evening lies, the fishermen
Overhaul their gear.

And the light receives
Blue overalls and black rubber boots
And drowns them sometimes in a wintry flash
From which they recover themselves, fastened by the usual thoughts
To the bobbing floats of their familiar heads,
And find again their own appearances.

Around them always is the sea:
And inside them with no murmur over the ground
The sea; and below, how do I know
How many fathoms down
Their trailing limbs go?
Into what fishtailed memory?

Seas in their heads, too; do they turn
Over in their beds with every ebb and flood?
Their sleep wide-open weather
Where fish swim and birds cry
Over and around them and inside them forever?

So not as men only but living up and down
Their obscure spirals of air and water they
Add their little rhythms to the sea,
Each man an estuary.

Yes, almost unhumanly,
Almost finned and winged as fish and fowl,
Almost as certain as they
In their own elusive counterpoint they move out,
Not to collide with but to ride
All rhythms and forces
As centaurs, horses themselves, ride horses.

But so incessantly
Do they need to retrieve themselves from drowning
In boats, in thoughts, in seas outside and in, however,
They become aware, they know terror
As the other pulse, the greater.

And they dare not eavesdrop on themselves, they dare
Not look within where all the underworld
Is turning into myth
In lust and dream, in drama and terror,
All that they are
To utter you who are unutterable:
You, caught up like a breath,
The very last before death.

2

Men with meanings
Inside that wait like cold wicks in oil,
Here they endure the wide stare of things
Roosting like seabirds, here they pull
Themselves out of the waters to keep station
On you like some continuous intimation:
Do you know them from other birds who fold their wings
Above the coasts and rain down droppings?

Are you always arriving ashore
And through them up some old waterstairs of feeling?
Are you the Igniter who climbs up the tower
Of their graze to light that archaic reeling
Lanthorn in each face?
Are you that cold thing in the gaze?
That barbarous look of the older climate
The halfmade man, the not-yet-private?

The fisheaters, the fishcatchers
Who rise arrayed in and shedding scales like
Electric shocks, who disappear for days into the weathers
Of the Giant's house, but to ride
Out when all is lost to dodge upon
An immense and dangerous horizon
And only when we've lost all hope
Come home on a fair wind up the telescope?

Poem for my Mother

1

That dismal country, Killimore-daly:
When my mother talks I know the place at once
And the faces of a century
All dead, but household gossip since;
And again she is my
Dream and my anatomy;
And my geography's that low blue knoll
Over the bog where the black miles are all
To the sky's far wall.

The first on her tongue is that gentle and precise
Grand-uncle James. He tilled the arable
And was a sacrifice
To ties I'd think intolerable.
He was a second son; and one night
When his elder brother's horse took fright,
The cart upturned, and with his brother dead
He found himself with a family ready-made;
And no woman in his bed.

A homely stately man, with an old oaken
Dignity and a courtly way of speech
That left unbroken
The delicate things in a child's reach:
To six girls he was
More than their looking-glass;
And I with my mother's eyes upon me see
The simple and major figure she'd wish on me,
The father I refuse to be.

James was a Dilleen. My mother's mother's people
Were the fair-haired Burkes from the bridge at Raford;
Millers whose old green wheel
Still grinds for a neighbour's board;
Beech and the bubbling poplar
Ride up the small trout-water
To the sheltered slates where once a harsh-faced wife,
Frank Burke's second woman, spent her life
And her good man's in strife.

A family legend, she; not kind it seems
To step-children. There was some whispered talk,
So my Grand-uncle James,
The sturdy man, in his riding cloak
Rode out one winter night
To do the thing was right;
He downfaced the woman on her hearth, he took
The child from the coals and wrapped it in his cloak;
Her lullaby his gentle look.

Pride of that night-ride's in my mother's eyes
When she talks of it. I hear the horse-hooves on
White frost, the stars and trees
Are Christmas; in the lamp six girls listen
And open the door to a call
To take a child like a doll
From an old man's arms – no, not a doll, a rose;
Rose of his heartbeat, as if his life's repose
Had flowered in his frozen clothes.

2

But the woman of the mill, that temper on a hair
And the pride that's an appetite for self-destruction,
She's the one lays bare
The bones of chronicles: no ruction
But the terrible cerebral itch
Of a self-regarding bitch
Will not stir up, as if she found each place
Dull as a mirror, but in all wild displays
The life inside her face.

The Mill landlord was a jackboot in
The older style, but fair. He called one night
And asked Burke for possession
Of a park he'd leased. He'd all the right,
So Burke agreed. But the door
Opened and his wife with a glare
That silenced him, strode in convulsed and red
And threw a bag of sovereigns at his head:
Fight the bugger, she said.

Take this, the whole strongbox, and till it's spent
On law I'll never have enough of law,
Says she, O the termagant.
And law she had till out-at-elbow,
With Frank dead and the rent
Overdue, she went
Out of the chronicle to America;
Unmourned, unhonoured, even disliked in her day,
But a person in her own way.

She touched her time, but never the people; strange
For her quarrel was the quarrel of the time
When a land-squabble could arrange
Banners and processions and walk out in rhyme:
Does the country, in one who struts,
Guess the illness in the guts
Seeking a tall and suicidal end?
Whom the gods wish to destroy will find no friend
Where all are wise and bend.

3

She was a figure of pride. There was another
Not far away, one of the quality;
And he, says my mother,
Had all the country's sympathy,
His name was Dominic John
Burke-Browne, a gentleman
Of blood so ancient it had lost the sting;
His home was a Norman keep, a naked thing;
The house a plastered wing.

Two sisters, spinsters, this proud bachelor had
With vague accomplishments. In rainy grandeur
One of the two went mad
And wandered the callows with goose and gander:
And when they'd drag her home,
Her neck stretched out in the spume
Of an angry goose, she'd hiss, they say. The other
Had buried her youth without much fuss or bother
And liked that Burke my grandmother:

So much that from the castle the soft fruit came
In baskets down the lane on summer days
From a Burke to a Burke, poor name
That used such different umbrellas;
And, gesture from kin to kin,
A man with a delicate cane
And the carpet walk of the sheltered bookman trod
The winter time up to his heels in mud
That the royal thing confer with its blood.

Old privilege, though he was a Catholic,
Had made it customary he should pray
Curtained away from Mick
And Pat on Sunday and Holyday;
But some Maynoothman with
No reverence for myth
Ruled that all men when down upon the knee
Before the Lord were the one family tree;
And took away his canopy.

He never passed the font again, they say:
And strangely no one blamed him. They had pity
For the proud old man on Sunday
For there in one high window he
Was seen to raise the glass
When bells rang out for Mass
And face the little chapel over the trees,
Missal in hand, upon his bended knees.
And no one felt at ease.

O the stories told about him. There were three
Fools in the parish, three old brothers who
Stole turf nightly;
And wondering if it were true
They were such fools, he set
A trap for them, he put
A crown-piece on a style between the quicks
They'd need to climb to play their usual tricks
On his Nobility's turfricks.

They came at dawn, sluggards, one, two, three
Homespun men, the eldest first as of right;
He passed unseeingly;
But the second saw it – and with no second sight:
Wondering, gibbering, he
Showed it and the three
Filled a pipe and passed it round and round.
To contemplate the better what they'd found,
They sat upon the ground.

A silver piece, and it could have been the moon
That had fallen down for all the complicated
Wonder it brought them. One
By one the younger were animated;
But the eldest, a man of laws,
Pondered all his saws
Till he found that which removed perplexity;
Says he, to each day that day's task, if it be
The turf today, then tomorrow we'll gather money.

The crown was returned to its place, the moon to the air,
And one by one they climbed in their innocence
A style and a townland's laughter.
But O Dominic, man of sense,
Were you the wiser, you
Who gave yourself to the blue
And bookish fiction and denied the red
Blood that clamoured for a girl in bed
And bedamned to the esquired dead?

What had you, O delicate hail-fellow to a book,
More than those slovenly louts who warmed their shins,
You, too, on the hook
Of a logical witless innocence,
You shown the chapel door
By a world you knew no more.
Your dispensation done, who yet strove still
To live your lie, who never lived your will,
Upon your purple hill?

So much for Dominic Burke-Browne. He died
When my mother was young, and some herdsman moved in
And never, they say, thrived.
A place to end, not to begin;
An inimical place
To people born on the grass
Whose business is weather and the tillage patch,
All the simple traffic that needs no latch
Between fields and the thatch.

Ghosts, says my mother; and perhaps the dead can throw
Shadows sometimes that the living see.
One is a Dutchman who
Got the castle after Aughrim as his fee;
Not to enjoy it forever;
One night in an embrasure
When he struck a spark to light his pipe the wall
Glowed like a Dutch interior, and some tall
Burke blasted him with a musket ball.

She names ghosts one by one in her chronicle.
One story's funny. Three men sought shelter there;
Two were tall, so the middle
Of the bed was the small man's share;
All night his sleep was lost
For some Euclidean ghost
Whose delight was symmetry tugged till his feet lay
By the tall man's feet, then after some delay
Violently tugged the other way.

5

Tale after tale she tells that brings me back
To a townland that's almost woman to me,
To the heart before the crack
To the peace before the poetry;
Back farther where the earth
Is my pre-natal birth,
Even beyond you, woman, who are tall
As the Mother of God, to your own watery knoll,
So blue where black miles are all.

Between Attymon and Cloonshicahill, between
Lisduff and Brackloon, Woman, O my maid,
In a townland never seen,
When all townlands were in your head,
You must have imagined a son
And he when your time was done
And it was his turn to seek your face inside
Discovered not a mother nor a bride
But a living countryside.

In all the levels of my eye you are;
And I divine you, I, your diving fork;
O my discovery of water,
You always here where poems work.
No dwindling woman with
A worn face but the myth
That magnifies, hurts, and satisfies till all
My gaze is gathered up upon the tall
Mountain where Muses dwell.

Be there away, but mostly here beside
My blood, in the humdrum of your chair, be you
Most plainly and abide
As if the fire and lamplight too
Found you a resting place;
Mistress of my house, and let this room be kind
From gazing on you when I draw the blind
On the night outside my mind.

Pot Shot

I tell words that talk in trees, this hill
Is my vocabulary, and when I lie down
The sky seizes me so very quietly
I reflect the sunset, the river and I are one.
And then the gun goes off. Am I that, too?
Thunder and blast? And when the hooves of the echoes
Have galloped over the grass and the field aloofly
Returns to itself and silence on its toes
Cranes to hear a rabbit squeal, am I
The wound that I give, the hurt I hurt, the shiver
That talks so tall in trees, that is the sky,
That explodes in death, yet walks like the wide river
So calmly through the evening that I tame
The world around me till it names my name?

Vowels

A: Watermaid, the frantic virgin who
Yet hides her birth where man must hatch it. E:
Distant and elongated drapery,
The lady-never-won whom all men woo.
O: midsummer woman, countryside
And sway, the opulent bed, the wed, the bride.
U: is my mother gathering up the view,
Majestic, with an apple on her knee.

But I: I, is my danger; my knotted thread
And needle's eye; my ancient grandmother
Who tells my follies while she sews my shroud.
At times she fades as if not made of matter,
And then again her glance is all a glitter
When she lifts her shears and chatters with the dead.

Dialogue Between Raftery and Death

Argument: Raftery the poet finds that his mistress, a married woman, is having an affair with a visiting sailor. The shock is severe and he considers death for the first time as a part of life. Tradition tells us that he saw the bony figure of Death one night in his room; and that he who was blind found his sight while the vision lasted. He denied this vision later, however, under pressure from the clergy, and I prefer to take it as I write it here.

RAFTERY: There is someone here?

DEATH: Yes, Raftery.

RAFTERY: I know the voice

DEATH: You know the voice.

RAFTERY: I do. It walks on all my drums. It fills me
          Fuller than my heart. I have such noise
          Inside me that the red rope of my pulse
          Rocks me like a bell-tower. Visitor,
          Are you inside or outside all my walls?
          Are you Raftery's angel, that wild trumpeter?

DEATH: No, Raftery. Never a trumpeter.

RAFTERY: Who, then?

DEATH: A Dignity that lacked a voice till this,
          And so long silent, you may call me Silence.

RAFTERY: You use an alias so, for Silence is
         The nightly gift this room gives Raftery.
         You have another name?
                 I need not delve.
         The steepletops are still, yet toll it slowly
         And all the clocks strike twelve.

         You are an angel of death?

DEATH: Yes, Raftery.

RAFTERY: A moment ago and I was throwing myself

16

From every tower. Now strangely I find dignity
Inside me once again.

DEATH: O, at the end it's natural
For Death to be received so quietly.
I am so quiet myself, indeed, I invoke
Quiet so palpable I leave it after me
As you might leave the scent of tobacco smoke
And, by the by, you smoke too much.

Raftery looks up for the first time

RAFTERY: And you
Are Death?

DEATH: Just your particular death.

RAFTERY: I'm honoured, by God.
I have a death the spit of Loss the grocer

DEATH: Now, more respect –

RAFTERY: O, all the pipes aboard
Will shrill for the admiral. But I'll have a death that look
Like Death and not like poor meek Loss, whose sister
Kept him collecting jumble clothes for blacks
Till he, too, went in dread of the human figure.

DEATH: I am what you have let me be. I, Death, am
The twin of Life, you know. With you we knit
In one and make you a person. And a nasty time
I've had of it, my twin your favourite
From the very first, never a thought for me;
Always ignored. And the house never quiet.
You two jaunting, drinking, bringing women home
And singing, dancing, raving, ranting; every night
Bright as a brothel; no thought for a nice quiet tomb.

RAFTERY: I do not believe it.

DEATH: What?

RAFTERY: That you are Death.

17

DEATH: I insist that you believe in me, Raftery. You must
Allow me at least the dignity of existence.

RAFTERY: Death imposes more. The Striker. What!
And the Strider of our dust.
The lightning flash, the thunder on the house.

DEATH: But I am – l mean I would be – I believe
I could be
Thoroughly terrifying …

RAFTERY: Maybe to a mouse …

DEATH: But you ignore me, and give me no chance, Raftery.
I've lived like a prisoner – no, an exiled Royalty –
Inside you, Raftery; downcast, downtrodden because
You would not even become aware of me;
Why, tonight's the first time you have loaned me a face
And what a face. Other men's deaths can wear
The loveliest frightful masks, but I have this
Parody as if you'd kicked my rear.
You are no gentleman, then a poet never is.
O, I was born unlucky. Give me a king
And I could be so vast and royal a shiver
All lamps would seek me out. A throne's the thing
For ghostly eminence. You've heard of Alexander
But never how night uncrowned him, how that
Conqueror
Who'd so much sun he'd scorch a neighbouring hamlet
Was after dark but a star-and-gartered nightmare
All the great Asian gutters running sweat.

RAFTERY: You do not listen?
Vanish, now, you interrupt me.

DEATH: But you called me.

RAFTERY: When?

DEATH: You wished to die.

RAFTERY: And God's grey footman ran obediently?
Is a lover allowed no rhetoric? What if I did cry?

DEATH: Must I leave emptyhanded?

RAFTERY: Take me then. Or try.

DEATH: You hold the ground
          Like a stone monument.

RAFTERY: Do I hear you sigh?

DEATH: I cannot move you.

RAFTERY: Vanish then, or not a sound.
          You interrupt my quarrel with the sky.

DEATH: Another squabble with God? The old story
          Of your soul, that trouble-the-house. If you had not a
                                                                soul,
          You'd still invent one, Raftery.

RAFTERY: Never. The soul ignites me
          Like a spill of paper. Who'd be the fuel
          Of a sky-climber only to go on fire?
          Soul burns everything, every love, it serves
          My body worse than a syphilitic father,
          A lunatic runs up and down my nerves.

          Can't I love without soul?

DEATH: Love. Love. Is the life principle
          One vast erection, a candle in a windy cave?
          You do not need this flary fellow –

RAFTERY: It is not sensible
          To burn like this. Every woman's a grave,
          And a corpse is all love needs. Yet Raftery
          Is wrung by some tall lunar thing, wings beat
          In heaven when he loves. O, Raftery
          Has too much of God for two clay feet.

          I put the case to Heaven. A man should walk
          Untouched from woman to woman and take his
                                                    pleasure.
          My text is lechery ...

DEATH: Jack Soul up his beanstalk,
          God's glittering gossip ...

RAFTERY: Every woman's a whore,
          And lust is enough, for the pain when it aspires ...
          Distraction of moonlight, the donkey gallops around,
          He brays from the grass, white rage to his flattened ears
          But the moon's no mare to be covered from the ground.

DEATH: You've taken up my theme and now you speak
          My life aloud. I'm the tired flesh inside
          Already muttering because trumpets break
          The lovely silence. The Soul will sound for pride,
          Go chiding, striding, in all its ignorance
          That we who're not combustible can tire
          Of wings and things and only ask the silence
          That lets us fall asleep about the fire.

RAFTERY: You are here still?

DEATH: Why, I'm stronger, now.
          Your flesh argues for me.

RAFTERY: Don't you know yet
          That every love invents me all anew?

DEATH: Nonsense. Your dreams unbuild you every night.
          You know you've too much wisdom to go on
          Enforcing Soul on the body, accumulating guilts
          For nothing. Why, even if you love this woman,
          She's only your death-wish walking round on stilts.

          I undermine you a little?

RAFTERY: I see you'll try
          Another tilt in a minute.

DEATH: I'm trying now,

RAFTERY: I scarcely notice.

DEATH: Raftery, that is a lie.

20

RAFTERY: A little lie, perhaps. You've found some power
You didn't have at first. It's not enough.

DEATH: But you're aware of me.

RAFTERY: I know you're here.

DEATH: The first black shadow. It's a curious stuff
That tailors itself; it's Life's black underwear.

I chill you a little?

RAFTERY: I stoke the fire
Just that little more. Do you go away?

DEATH: I stay, of course. Your Great Corrupter.
From this time on I lend you my strange eye.
A vision of acid, Raftery. You look upon
A face and the face turns blank, the marvellous living
Mask collapses on the skeleton
Before your eyes; and behind it – only nothing.

RAFTERY: Against that nothing, I can think of a face
That startles me, a woman's face that floods
My whole house with sun and tall stained glass …

DEATH: Against that nothing those few coloured muds
Are less than nothing. And the moody woman within
Already knows the hands of a certain tailor
And the garment he tailors, so she lives in sin
And tries to forget him with a common sailor.
But you know all this.

RAFTERY: I know it, O God.

DEATH: And still you live. And the sailor is still alive.
For all your poetry and frenzy, poet,
The seaman's got her. And still he is alive.
How the Liberties will mock you over the case.
Mock you more than that poor man, her husband;
The poet cast for a jockey of the high seas,
A high-rigged boy with a bellyfull of wind.

RAFTERY: I have no hangman's taste for certain neckwear.

DEATH: A lovely instrument. One string finds all
Silence in a note; an instrument for a lover
Since all great love is suicidal.
If you love greatly, then leave your love behind
Fixed like a stone, your wildness in a gesture;
Arrange it, Raftery, be forever self-contained;
Death is the measure of a lover's stature.
And the peace after the glory. To leave behind
A self in people's minds …

RAFTERY: The glory is the slut's
Who could excite such passion, and for the suicide
Peace is a burial with a stake down through his guts.

DEATH: But someone must die for love. It should be you
Who love love loudest.

RAFTERY: To sing love is my trade.
I'll go on singing if only to prove to you
A living poet is better than a dead.

I see you no longer.

DEATH: Do you mean, I can't be seen?
(faint)

RAFTERY: You've gone.

DEATH: I'm here, I'm here.

RAFTERY: And scarcely to be heard
Have I finished you?

DEATH: No. I'll be strong quite soon.

RAFTERY: Soon enough, when I'm whiskered and grey-haired,
A crutch in my hand and the priest beside my bed
And no tall woman smiles at me from a poem.
Where are you now?

DEATH: I think I'm – once more dead.

RAFTERY: Then let us call a general post-mortem.

Maud Gonne

1

Somewhere in this city
She must have left herself, somewhere
Left her heartbeat
In one tall rose of space;

Left herself, the whole
Body and glitter in a moment, like a niche,
Fixed there, gesture and all,
But living, living through every fingertip.

The passion still
A well, a vowel; through a lover or a thought
She streams in an endless jet against the will
Of time. I look for that wild silhouette

And bless the south and north and east,
The west where I was born I bless
That four impersonal mirrors may throw back at me
The sea-cold currents of her face.

2

Gods are our journey into space;
But here, if passion were high, a single flower
Offered to her might shake the place
With so much life your flower could disappear,

Yes, flowers could be taken from my hands and my hands talk
Back to me from wonder and miracle,
The space between hands and heart so tall with shock
Fingers scarcely know the girl.

Gods who transform the simple touch
Of lust are kind. O, out of the blue damps
Of Ireland this great ache in me must read
A face that will burn all my lamps.

She will be helmeted, outrunning her own hair
Serenely, winged with a large look.
Ah Christ, if one could scrape off time like paint
And for once just be moonstruck.

3

Trees and lawns at the windows.
An armchair. The fitful sleep. The tall clock ominous.
This is an old woman full of shadows
Returning to her eyes, who slowly becomes luminous.

This is the last of her, a still
Gaunt lamp of a woman with a wasting wick.
How calm is the face that burns the precious oil.
But I call on the girl within, I beckon the first face back.

And I think surely as I enter the courtyard
Of that large look and its paving of light, I need
Only a trumpet and the horned gate, Omega,
Would open wide to Alpha, the tall, the white-kneed.

I drop roses on the folded hands
And time receives them. O, let them fall far back
At the girl's feet where, stripped and full of fury,
She rages to scatter herself along the track.

4

The sculptors gather round her, the sculptors show
As she moves out of their hands into clay and bronze
Her public face of ravage and shadow,
A gaze that drops tears like stones.

A woman with a heavy reverie
Of tired eyes and the large loafing calms
Of age, a woman worn as history
With the world's lost causes pleading from her palms.

All the tired flourish ending in this stone
In a public square. That's what the woman in her
Who hated the woman wanted, it was her ambition;
And she has a kind of public life forever.

But O the revenge when the hands begin to dream
Of lovers she dented, the long dead,
And she cannot think for stone and the stars and the traffic stream
And the gulls that foul her head.

Leave her to us, the poets. We will make her
Litanies, and give our furies
A fulcrum that will lift and spread around her
Feelings like new territories,

This woman who knows no gravity
That waterfalls down the spine is not for you.
She is our story.
The sudden lifting of the brow.

She who inhabits a great lens
Like vision, who increases all our themes
Has left you nothing that can be touched with fingers
But something tall still walks into our poems.

And we fade through the lonely and passing phases of flesh,
And a silence sings. O tall moon on the hill,
Mother of trees and their slow striding,
Mother of towers that stand still.

6

And yet to create a way
Of words where she may walk into a poem
Is to deceive you, my heart, O red giant inside me.
Life, not death, should be our theme.

If rooms still beat like hearts, if silk speaks to me strangely
In the language of a body, it is one we cannot touch.
That way lies futility,
Better the tribal bitch.

Better the woman who loosens your great knots
Of muscle, giant, in all the hates of love.
Do not listen to the poets.
Love is only to be alive.

Love will sell you out. But even so you will
Still have your nature left for that last aloof
Moment when you leave the millwheel.
Enough, Samson, to shake down the roof.

Book of Job

The simple thing is to die
So often and so painfully that I
One day in one breath
May live the whole life of death.

The daily thing is to be
Defeated daily, that this psychology
Of victory be unlearned
And sham into shame be turned.

For this Image is not Me;
This worldling satisfied and stately, with his family
Thanksgiving, and each day success,
The world always answering yes.

In this gift of luck I have lost
The naked traffic of the ghost
Trapped in an image I projected
Not of God but God's elected.

So the next thing is to ride
Horse and all under and be no more a pride;
No, nor an humility,
For that's a pride too, on one knee.

But to be nothing till
Flesh fall off and my heartbeat sounds real;
Until my heart is heard
Stammering with excitement its one word.

Come then rags and plagues
I am honoured to lend you my legs;
Enter this suffering house
Where honours fall off, where I delouse,

And bless me no more, You
In the twittering evening: O tall fall of dew
You fathered me so much ease
I ponder all misery now to find my peace:

I have my occupation; I will die
Into nothing after nothing, but live no lie,
Stripped to a faint shiver, waiting here
On a faint illumination in the air.

A Flask of Brandy

You, said the Lionwoman,
Pliz, this errand, a snipe of brandy
From the first shop. Here's money;
And for you this penny.

And on my way I saw:
Item, a clown who waltzed on stilts;
A bear saluting with a paw;
Two pairs of dancing dogs in kilts;
Eight midget ponies in a single file,
A very piccolo of ponies;
Then the princess far off in her smile;
And the seven beautiful distant ladies:
And then –

Facing after the big bandwaggon, he
The boy in spangles, lonely and profound:
Behind him the Ringmaster, a redfaced man,
Followed by silence heavy as a wound,
And empty.

Quickly as two feet can did I come back
To the Lionwoman with her cognac.

You, said the Lionwoman;
Pliz to the window, said foreign gutterals in
The cave of the caravan.
I waited, errand done.

And waiting on one foot saw:
Item: a twitching coloured chintz
Moved by a lemontaloned claw:
And after a woman with her face in paints,
A throat thickened in its round of tan
On shoulders sick and white with nature;
Behind was a pair of bloomers on a line,
Blue; a table with a tin platter:
More else:

A black electric cat, a stove, a pot
Purring, and a wild Red Indian blanket
Crouching sidewise on a bunk;
And some exciting smell that stunk
Till the Lionwoman rising blotted out
All but a breast as heavy as a sigh
That stared at me from one bruised eye.

The Head

1

The day after decapitation
Was no wound yet. Noon found the head
Excited still and still singing
The visionary woman, still exalting
The woman in measures to which no words came
Off the black tongue. The river flies
Were busy on specks of blood, in clouds upon the hair;
But where her praise was fixed upon his face
No one had died, the flesh was adequate;
And on a mouth that seemed alive
Only the smile was anti-clockwise;
But no wound yet.

That night it drifted on
Through stars that buzzed no brighter, inches
Of radiance before it and around
That felt no wound;
And this was dyed with a flutter of vague moths,
And overhead where a curious white owl
Dilated, there was some reflection too;
And down below
More of it and stranger, for the eels
Had scented blood and wavered under the wicker;
This was a head that trickled down many tails
Into the deeps, eddying without end;
And still was felt no wound.

The slow morning came
Back to the eyes and brought the labouring crow
(Corvus corax corax) who discharged himself
Upon the skull unskilfully and cawed
Once, twice, and there for long was still.
The gulls disturbed him when the eyes were gone
And over the bloody mess rose such confusion
Three salmon fishers rowed out from a draft
Only to retch their morning stirabout:
That noon the skull gaped
And still was felt no wound.

The second afternoon it rained;

Rinsing the ruin the nozzled drops removed
Sundry strips, tissues, barber's clippings,
Odds of nerves, bits, leaving such scrags, jags
And rags as still clung and dripped
To shine strangely when the sun came out.
The waters steamed a little before night
And from the skull where little pools remained
There oozed a smoke, a vagrant and hairlike smoke;
And in the hollow eyes the rain
Was bright as sight, and so it seemed
The nose put forth its bridge again,
And from the earholes arched two tufts of fawn
Two gilded wisps, the ears. The face had dreamed
Itself right back again.
And still no pain;
Still the exultant thing was fixed, and dawn
Found the bare teeth beautiful.

The third day repeated as before
Washed out the skullhouse and refurnished it
With the changeable midsummer weather:
The head alone at last
Was bonebare and beaming; and where it floated
Down the broad vowel of the river, once
Its song was heard;

Snatches only, faint upon the ripple
And weirs of the water-word: a thin
Piping.

The reeds heavytopped tipped to it
As to a breeze.

                              So it was the wind
That used the tattered wizen of the throat
As well as the sockets of the eyes, the earholes
And the pit behind the nose for hollow music,
Not overlooking the jewels of the mouth
That still smiled
For yet no wound was felt.

So time stopped
Outwardly, but there was still this woman
In the weather of the head
Who was all time to it no longer human.
And in that time the head came

By stages of water world
From green granaries, tilled, from fat uddered
Cow-lawns by river houses, woods that spoke in oak
And heavy roots and clumped along the banks
To a country narrow low and cold
And very thin like a wire,
Where the head sang all day.

There the seas fell inland almost vacantly
Over a sieve of sand;
There the head lay
While the coracle under it of sally withes
Dried, withered in sunlight, salt sealight,
Rotted till the ashen thwart that held the head
Rigid and singing, sprung the spent lashings,
Tipping over;
This, one day when the set from the southwest
Piled up an equinoctial on the coast;
On the white shore with no one to notice
The head fell.

And broke

In a separation of its major and distinct parts.
Two.

And from the still centre where was the true
Bubble or heartbeat, came the tiny whimper
Of some unhouselled thing;
The head's first cry
At last and never heard

By gull, gale, sandpiping bird
Or gannet in the tall and touselled blue,
Nor the wader on two pins nearby,
Though the cry was human,
The pain spreading greatly, going
Towards blood in every direction

But never arriving
Near and away where the woman was
Doing the usual things to men and clothes
Afraid of the glass,
Groundswell and undertows,
What happens and the happening
That will never come to pass.

Coastal Waters

Holy Well

In the annals saints
Sit in holy wells, talk freely
To grim hermits, heal
Who ails, the foot-holy
Pilgrims who walk in wishes.

The dumb speak, the cripple
Walks, the blind
Find the dazzling world of the mind
In new pigments. Here
The ways of God seem wayward but very clear.

Speak the word, Saint,
In your welling mineral
That world in a bright and single jet
Go up, and inside it, lit up,
God my space and my material.

The Dwelling

At night the house grows
Around the blackshawled woman. Harsh
And sparse the bony room
But with the lamp
All the pieces give their lights:
She shines among her satellites.

Man-chairs of oak, scrubbed; a rack
Of cups and blue plates;
The tabled jug:
The oilcloth spreading from the wick;
The spindled stair without a rug
But scrubbed, scrubbed to the quick.

The tiny window's shut its eye;
Let the strand roar
And the white horses tumble on the shore,
Here catgreen
The salt driftwood purrs inside the fire
And the sea ends that pours around the world.

Somewhere an old working clock,
Weights and chains, ticks on and tells
The woman's hours;
The wether's wool in the knitted sock,
The world weather in
Her knotted face, her knotted talk;

How men come home
From the ocean drip, still rocking, ill at ease
Till she gathers them;
Here she sets them down in peace
Inside the lamp, the house, the shawl.
Here is the centre of them all.

And all the pieces hang
In one. The man is on the chair
Who winds the clock
Who'll climb the stairhead after her,
Adjust the wick
Till the great night idles, barely ticking over.

Day Ashore

Sundays the long boat of the week
Is drawn up, turned keel over on the sand;
Rest, fellows, on the old
Wall, bellying the wind.

Here the sea colour shoals
And the Pole fails to pull. Rest, fellows,
On your rock pillows
And the small seas that sleep in shells.

Tomorrow the heave as earth turns over
Into Monday. Take your ease.
Light the pipe. Sit on forever.
Forget you're cold saltwater to the knees.

Love

1

The strong man
Is he only after all the creature of what seems
Desirable, whom nothing else can
Please because once it was all the boy's dreams?

A girl on a horse
In the leaves of autumn, in the careless havoc of the air;
Behind her over the lawn the big house,
And she prouder for that house there.

Magnificent the dream
To the boy who peers from the wall. She gallops on
But never away, the house there all the time,
Skies unmoving, the journey never done.

2

Ring out
Bells, give the lads a holiday;
Shutters down and shops shut, a stout
In every fist. It's love will find a way.

Love, or its dunce
The desperation that throws in its hand
Before the miracle happens that for the nonce
Will open up the land.

Is it always she,
The first, the almost forgotten, some ancient lie
That shattered us with truth, who is the enemy
And must be triumphed over for the boy?

Bless them. Ring, Bells.
They are what they are, they have what they have, enough
For whom the bell tolls
To tell their desperate stuff.

Peasantry

In a thatch
That could be a stable but for the open hearth
A man is born, the tiller of the earth.
Labour there, dumb brothers,
And have no wild itch
To raise yourselves. The world is to your betters.

In the mall,
Discreetly behind curtains, servants wait
On money that makes itself early and late;
And with the cash goes credit
And breeding, all
Ripening of the person. This the rich inherit.

Walk the town,
Tiller, interloper, up and down, we
Who live upon you will allow this free,
But close our heavy doors
To any clown
Born to the thatch in the boor-stink of the byres.

The Poems of Love

All the poems of love are one;
All women too. The name that runs
Profanely between love and lover
Is the name repeated over
In the rosaries of nuns.
All the poems of love are one.

Solar red, masochist black,
There's precedent for each in heaven;
Whatever be a body's leaven
The rosaries of the holy nation
Thrill to some transfiguration.
Love makes up the thing we lack.

All the women Tom and Jack
Buy or bed, the slumtown tits,
Have bright otherworld habits;
A queen shares pillows with a clown,
Still nebulously wears her crown,
And is most royal on her back.

When Tom and his hedge mistress come
Drunken to the judgement seat,
The obscene measures on his tongue
Start the heavens into song;
Endlessly must Tom recite
The love he made by rule of thumb.

And brawling face and bawling gums
Fade fawnlike into some young grace;
Love lives serenely many ways;
Love lives in all that it may not lack
Its body in riots, drunks and drums
And the rosaries of nuns in black.

Meeting

Countryman, consumptive;
Some children, four, I believe;
Now burned by a sun of another colour,
Tells me again good-morning – sir.
This is truth, too, in one posture.

And easily related
To something already much stated
But always forgotten till a feeling thinks for me
The moment-to-moment philosophy
Of my overpressed mortality.

It does not moralize,
This feeling, but accepts that a man dies,
Daily and wearily; the portents are too plain,
Time running out through every vein,
The face the terminus of pain;

Continuously arriving there
Without shock and secretly, but almost bare
And terrified already. I could stand
And talk of seasons and the land,
But he'd see through me and understand.

And hear under my breath
Words that condole with my own death
That seems so distant now, and hear me too
Sounding the bull-head of my strength, anew:
Spitting where he must swallow down the chew.

Field Observation

There died last night
In a poor thatch that whiskered heavy man
Who used to go my road
Peaceful as Saturn and as countrified;

In a flit of moonlight,
With the town dwarf complaining in his sleep,
He left corpse and corner,
A broken pot and one bright glass of water.

No more will all things cast
His measure, horoscope or the great size of his breath,
Who was each year reborn
In the annual excursion of the corn;

Who moved in the gravity
Of some big sign, and slowly on the plough
Came out anew in orbit
With birds and seasons circling him by habit;

Morning fell upon
His horses, and the weather moved behind;
From cold Christmas he
Moved up the hill in every leafing tree.

Now the windy fallow
For harmony must invent him in its turn
Whiskers, seeds and eyes,
His bags about him and his flapping skies;

One day the low-fired sun
In hedges bare and barbed as rolls of wire,
An old stiff half-rayed figure, the sole reason
For each divulging season;

In hayloads lost in June, in
Autumn the wheaten man, while
At their harps together
His strawpale daughters tinkle in the weather;

No other kin, not one
Beam from the blues in the cold cowyards round
The mountain where the crows knew him but never
The women clinging to the winter flaws;

And leaves no name
A season won't erase, old Walrus-face
Who lined the surging team
On a long furrow straight as the morning beam.

Johnstown Castle

1

The summer woods refuse to meet
Us on the levels we know. We have evolved
Too much mind for them, and picked up feet
That solve things differently, like birds:
Trees use the old vocabulary
In all its ponderous gravity;
We with inner needs to be resolved
Have learned all the new and air-borne words.

Why intrude here, and why regret
An old root that like a rocket goes
On exploding season after season
In the same galaxy of leaf, without a reason?
All it knows
Is the old wholesome suit of clothes:
Never the new and complicated rose.

2

An ornamental water
Should be backed with mercury that the sculptured swan
May be ideal swan forever.
Here one shiver shows the mud
And I am glad because a swan
Can turn up his end and shatter mood
And shatter mirror,
Till the woods massed in an architecture shake
Because a real swan mucks up a lake.

An old lady, slender as her wand
Of ebony, and carrying her castle still about her,
Is near me anywhere I stand;
My own creation.
I give her words to say, and a world, too,
Homelier, perhaps, than that she knew,
And take an interest in the conversation:
But as I ramble on
Creating all for her
I think how certainly she lived this view
Merely by walking over the ground
Day after day; I falter
For now my words take on another hue
And such a sound
I'm half afraid to turn around.

Always my own monologue
Intrudes; things work into the word
Only to be imprisoned, or kennelled like a dog;
So the tall pine describes
A straight line up to the tuft of foliage
That sits it like a bird
And is only so much language
Because I use the word;
And all the ponderous oaks and the ooze underfoot,
All the harsh nerves of an old wood
That are a rumble in the nether-gut,
Are not what one transcribes
And never any good;
The monologue intrudes, my words let me
Into a poem, not into the poetry.

And yet a man must walk
Out of his mystery, if he's to meet it
Face to face, in talk,
And guess from words omitted the major and delicate
Evasions of his ghost
Who is the host
To every massive feeling and must live it.
Create me, says the poet, I am a body
For every word, the large word that was lost
And the word you'd throw a dog;
Transform me who travel towards infinity
In a makeshift monologue.

A Look in the Mirror

Those iron men!
The Indian wings his way upon an arrow;
Pale blue the sailor
Saunters on the sea;

And the farmer's boy,
Drinking his diesel, eats up the earth,
Spitting out the stones:
These never dwindle down in ink;

Nor Million Dollar
Heavyweights, nor does the Spaceman thrown
Against the dartboard of the moon,
For theirs are necessary capers;

These are the lovely eternal brutes:
All time's bravura, the hailed and the well;
Let us drink to them a foam of ale;
And in the glass consider you

Whom some half truth stuns
Now autumn ravishes; yet still possessed
By the savage script of the young man,
By the savage dictation,

A heart out of plumb,
And time out of mind, his head
Turned back on his shoulders, nodding
To a drunken line.

A question then,
Why thumb a disconsolate nose
At these marvellous fellows, you with that in-looking face
Your own mirror hardly knows?

1

All men rage in royal Lear
Poor old man,
His winter body out of plan,
His flesh antediluvian;

Knowing the perishable year
Is every old man,
And human nature out of date,
Yet clinging to the butcher's meat.

The head that guttered in the air
Is every old man
Nailed to the body, that bare tree,
Lost in the mutter of geography.

The mad white head, distracted stare
Is every old man
And fellow traveller, burnt out
And come into his second sight.

Leaves afterglows, the borrowed wear
Of every other man,
The raiment of an old mad king,
Some tattered daft Platonic thing.
All men rage in old mad Lear.

2

We put James Starkey down today,
A few of us old friends and went our way;
The last, said we;
Gone the galaxy.

March Twentysix, a raindown day;
A blackbird yielding to one single spray;
Delicate the flute
Lifted above the mute.

Poi s'ascose nel foco
Che gli affina – there too without echo,
Sweetly undone,
Is Lesbia's sparrow, the little one.

No sweet mouth but comes to this,
God Attis too for all that Great Goddess
And heavenly stuff:
Much is man and not enough.

River Lane

1

That girls in the river, nymphs
Aloof in the female whorl and seashell shiver,
Could ever become old women beating clothes!
That those gay whipsters, virgin born
Tuning the milkwhite unicorn
Under the singing linnet at lane doors
Should turn to old mad gossips thumb to nose.

That our Madge who had such bubble and bud
Into her latest motherhood
Forgetting that the body's lent,
Should prolong the happy time of rut,
A great bulldozing Bacchic slut
All anguish when her time was spent,
Still clinging to her instrument;

All the passions come to stay;
In love or out of it no holiday.
With little left, the wick is all.
Ridiculous Helen will blue the moon
With the shadow of her going down;
Leda in her dotage scull
A mess of feathers on a pool;

And our old drunken Madge sail out
To bully the babble in the common street;
In the square no less, filled with the itch
And opulence of the vanished myth,
And suffering some kind of death,
Shake her clothes off every stitch
To show the roses of the bitch.

What lover ever who threw on this peg
A coat of arms could sing the wagging dug,
Or see the seaborne for the crows,
Or know for truth that on this breast
Man runs, a vast historic beast,
His race between her mouth and knees
And shoots his arrows at her skies?

Precisely under the church clock
She spins for all eyes round the Zodiac.
The world stands still
While she unlocks the raven hair
In the lost youth that envelops her.
Percussion of pigeons on the chapel bell:
The town one worldwide windowsill.

A little quiet country place
Shattered by an old mad mask of savage face;
Venus Anadyomene
Gone screwy, with every churchman's shaft
Feathering her broomstick tuft;
Careless of councils and decrees
The pigeons flutter round her knees.

She has the square to herself,
Old Madge, fallen off the wagon, and off the shelf
Where the cruse of oil is rich
With the Virgin's face, and history is not
The crescent that grows and ranges round the lot
To finish its moon round such,
Occulting on a cratered crutch.

Yet a most sonorous whore;
An excess of flesh; the epic had its hour.
And now like bats she calls her twittering dead
To beak and nuzzle, the horsed Huzzar
Or maybe her first conqueror,
That Esquire in his hunting red
Who drank from her uplifted head.

2

Piously
They say; a Rosary
In the flagrant hands; the treed God
On the gargantuan deserted mamillae:

From her house of finches,
Shouldered by six goes
Her piece of pine;
We take it in turns, each man to his trick;

She's rights in the old graveyard, so
It's round the town for us, an ancient custom;
My right shoulder aches at the stone cross;
The old drumbeat was a weight;

And I doubt if she's yet translated
From that batwinged virago, akimbo
In her bawling shawl;
The gates are open and we trample in

Where the de Burghs lie under broken
Slabs. Glass wreaths
Crunch on unkempt graves. It's noon
When we reach her upturned pile and pay her down.

Not a sob, not a face breaks, she'd gone
Far past her span, gone on, gone on
With the untimely rhetoric
Of a mastodon.

The first spadeful; a shake
Of holy water from a naggin bottle,
A Pater and Ave. (Though she died in a Mary habit
Nobody thinks she'll make it.)

Noon, and in the spare woodwork
Of December, low
As a lilac blooms suddenly the sun;
And I think maybe she did and all:

For what man ever
Quite totted up the human figure?
Here's famous holy ground at least,
And she lies at long last with the great.

The River Walk

Disturbing it is
To take your stick sedately walking
Evening in the water and the air,
And discover this; that a woman is a river.
The mythic properties are hard to bear.

Dismaying are
The ways she will intrude – if she intrude
Or merely assume the garments that you give her:
But a water willow stared at for so long
Glows graciously and knows the why you brood.

And such gesticulation –
Are you so young? – before the gentle birch
In its first shimmer: Lover, are you true
To one, or merely finding all you search
Brings the one woman home to you?

But how absurd to see
Her in that stilted bird, the heron in
A silt of river, all her blues pinned up:
In that brocaded goose the swan
For all her myths with Jupiter on top.

Dangerous, dangerous
This mythology. The doctors know it
And reason of it now like any poet.
Lover, go back no farther than your birth:
A woman is a woman, not the earth.

Her human business is
To resolve a man of other women always,
Not be, in a beautiful grotesque, all bodies
So various, a lover – if the girl insist
On love – must be a very pantheist.

A Public Appointment

He was stranding on the ripple
When she looked, the virgin. Her mute maids stood
Broadbeamed in the morning, washed, and nude as ingots,
While she went on.
The thing before her was no monstrous shell,
But a red man run over by the ocean.

She was to learn that pity was a pity
Between a man and a woman, but could she then, a virgin,
Know it, whose body heavenly Athene
Used so subtly
To break down this bull-man to her own
Particular lust– that's beyond flesh and bone?

So what the hero saw
In his run-down vision while his footsteps ranged
Around him uncontrollably as dolphins,
Was the white tower she was
And the sacred woman
In the city inside the city, unsacked Ilium.

Lustres he'd lost at sea
Would come back, he'd borne such brunts before
On his wide sea-front and taken them for granted;
But this was a new peril,
And in his weakness sweeter than the Siren,
This pity she offered him, so sisterly, so virgin.

The first look had made them
All ever they could be to one another,
Suppliant to Goddess, son to mother;
Neither was aware
Of all that was lost
Though it wept and swooned around them in the ghost.

And the girl had felt
The male in the storm that breached him, the rough pelt
Of the lover, and all the rolling bed.
But the man was down
Below the mercury; undone.
The great boomerang remained unthrown.

So Pallas Athene had her way.
Ulysses, recovered from the ocean and the blue
Barbarous tattoos of the receding god,
Was returned posthaste
To his public appointment. All
In heaven and earth bow down to protocol.

Yet when his people, shepherds
With heads in the clouds and sailors pouring water,
Demanded a statue to that sacred eloquence,
What rose up in the square
Was not oracular, no great mouthing of stones,
But the wanderer, that slender buffeted bronze.

Yes, though he died old and slowly
Into his vineyards, requiring like the sun
One whole horizon to decline upon,
The image that remains
Is the haunted man on the main of love, forever
Sailing, and beside him a virgin at the tiller.

An Island

A man must go naked to an island,
Let the weather lend
A skin till he grows one, the rock fit
The beat of the surftop to
His feet; let him go like spindrift
Till he find wings, or the wave
Streamline him like the great
Matter of a seal.

Let him find toes too,
Prehensile or web, for the cliff fall;
Let him put two notes in his pipe
And be the first music.
Let the island be the eye
And the boundary of his being, then
Let him be an island
And bound on his own beat,

Back before Gods,
Before the beginning, before the betrayal,
Before the woman slopped over on his bed,
Before the sun stood on a stone circle;
Let him go back to be
Just one simple thing, matter, an island
At its first meeting with the sea.

Weir Bridge

The lodestoned salmon, hurtling
Always in the right direction, find
The trickle of their birth,
Stand fantailed on the falls
And somersault into the milting weather.

Whole gravels are in rut.
The ocean has come home to melt away
The salt, to lie under
A maybush and almost tenderly
Suck from the lazy heavens a blue-green fly.

On love's seething house,
Rocking the thousand cradles, the first fresh
Will fall and the spent bulls
Drop with it down the slow river spirals;
Aching for space now the once rampant males;

Caught here in their bored
Congregations, while the wandering nerve
Twitches towards Norway. How many years
Since I first saw the stones waver,
The river paving turn to fins and tails?

Loafing a lunch hour in the sun,
And here's the wheel come round again;
So much to do, so little done;
The tiny trickle of my birth
Dwindling back into the earth.

Gowran Park, Autumn Meeting

The year's potatoes, they've ploughed them out,
The threshing rig's gone round about;
Earth finishes with the harvest time.

A low sun noses through the damps;
The trees are bare down to the stumps;
A mist can spring up white as lime.

The fox is red as the huntsman's coat,
The doublebarrel rhymes a note,
The season turns on the hill;

But day sits up like a hunkered hare
As horse and jockey catch the roar;
Gowran lights like a paper spill.

Soon long shadows will creep from the grill
Of every gate, the mountains stamp,
The year fall into the Christmas lamp.

The Young Fenians

They looked so good;
They were the coloured lithographs
Of Murat, Bernadotte and Ney
And the little Corsican.
Mars had made them from our dead
And given to each his martial head.

The cavalry and plumes would come,
No doubt about it;
Every half-acre man with a sword,
The boy with a drum;
And down the Alps of every local hill
The bannered horses ride to kill.

O'Connell helpless in the house;
The old gazebos at their talk,
All to no purpose;
Tone must rise and Emmet walk,
Edward troop out of Kildare;
The time had come; the day was fair.

Flags flew from our every word;
The new names sang from litanies,
Saviours each one;
They were the eagles in the morning sun;
A country rising from its knees
To upset all the histories.

Capricornian

In a quiet place,
Sea-locked, the moon is the pendulum
And the year the only face
Scanned for time;
The figures turn through the sun
Twelve ancients stand on the horizon.

Nearer than the twelve
Gazebos in their old star houses
Is the ram that rounds his horn on the hill;
The stone donkey by the wall
Is humble, has no wings; Taurus
Never stamped a cow like my black bull;

And my mother goat steps daintily
From ledge to ledge, ignores the fabulous
Ocean; she
Too is no heraldry, offers us
A full udder to fill the cans and
Occasionally brings forth twins

The old people love
To dine on, like
That old poet with his Falernian. He, too,
Found spring wells holy, some
God hung above
The natural bubble, his bright kingdom come;

Feared the sea god
Who locks havens, the sky piled
With wilder fellows, the uncontrollable;
Yet on a May day from the gorse
The eyes see fairly
A peopled sea, the hulls in a haze of morse;

And from our wedge
Of world, here on the very edge
Feel the one and the various move upon the spindle,
But the god singular,
An islandman
Who touches the chimney pots with smoke, who is a calendar

Of everyday affairs, a neighbour's voice,
A woman at the churn,
A child in wonder at the half door,
The split pollock drying in the sun,
The boats pulled up and
All night the moon, the pendulum.

A Visit West

1

The town is an ideogram
Of a town with its square keep and the brush of smoke
From the baker's chimney,
Almost intact at first sight
With wall and moat and narrow gate.
The wooden horse is in the square.

Everywhere my uncle Ben
Emerges with a limp from a round tower;
And that's the poem I'd like to write,
The old boy tipping his rod to the wavy weather,
Fish hooks and feathers thrown
Over the windy edge of March;
He owns them all now, the streaming rivers
By inalienable right.

So humbly down the river lawn
I'd tail him with a tuppenny pole;
(Hare's Ear, March Brown)
Here was a soul who lived alone;
Gone before I'd reach the bridge
Far off on a desolate slab of sky
Tipped off the harsh Atlantic roof,
Fly size.

The wooden horse is in the square.
Urbs, they say, intacta, meaning
The virgin sleeps late;
Between yawns life goes on
With some cunning to
Accomplish itself.

Children are born,
To up and vanish like me,
Mostly;
There is no return, and the wound
There and leaching
Forever into the one and
Only summer;

Lost.
The wooden horse is in the square;
And Ben, old Ben.

2

To pay off the ghost, two
Bottles of brandy
Left with the nuns to dole out
Circumspectly;
White coif and wimple, heavenly
Barmaids.

What greater wrong could I have done
On this cantankerous spirit
Limping in from nowhere with nuts and trout
And wild apples
Who'd get most nobly drunk on a market day!

What now he's gone?
New slates and paintwashed shops,
A garage in a flower bed;
Hovel and seeding thatch swept from the lane
And the hag's head
Curing slowly on
The smoking half door, like ham.

3

He saw a lingering eighteenth century out,
The great mansions left
Embedded in the prosy land
Die of their heraldry;
Even saw the last rebellion start,
The wooden horse stand in the square.

And never gave the world a thought
As the vast familiar glacier melted down;
While Kaisers fell and navies sank he drowned
His pint glass in Glynn's
Tallied his ewes abroad, his dog
Tucked at his heel, the West
Tumbling over him, his own sky
Strung from his fist.

Original
Inhabitant or feckless double
Opting out with his toy town and
Baby river,
An old primitive do-nothing who
Stabilised among the lesser shades
Can still pull

Me over the Shannon to lose me in
His greenery where the grass
Watches of the fields are stalled
Forever

And time is March and bright
Elysium
Where he disappears, his body gone
Into the weather
Without a care.

The wooden horse stands in the square.

Boyne Valley

On a mound chipped
From the dead, deity
And scantlings dismantled, the spell broken,
I stand on a stone ship
That sails nowhere

But once was set right to launch
The bronze and brandished hero, fellow
Of this same sun that low now
In bare twigs
Lies lumped in the winter's wicker basket,

Who was laid in
This hill of metaphor, as if a grave has no end,
Suspended in some state of grace above
His own diving depths
To find North like the barnacle

And a quite definite eternal Paradise
(Only the best admitted, Stags
Of the year, Gods
In the demi-brackets) not very different from this;
But Paradise is always somewhere else,

Leaving his head to the stone axe, and the big, broken
Torque of his body to dangle,
Wail, ye women,
God is dead
And picked over by this year's summer students,

Whose secret name was
A flight of months, the whole earth offering
Its barbarous alphabet to make him delicate;
Now trees and stones have forgotten; the birds
Are entirely without auspices

And preen flit strut in winter attitudes,
Birds, not litanies. The thing is gone
Now that no giant drops from the gaudy zenith
Like Mad Sweeney
To hang on the last Elder tree head and antlers.

Flayed, to be scattered in this the thirteenth
Unlucky month, for Fertility, for a patch
Of emmer barley, for all men –
To give their guts literally to this, –
To Demeter the first plough.

A sow, snouted with the moon's horn! But
It's Isis I think of, Magna Mater, to whom
The divine members from their schism clambered;
Into the magnet they came, the brilliant head
Topping the whole winged tread again –

Meaning just a new sun
On the old wheel, the one wheel, and world safe inside
The big roll of gravity, but
Aware there is a moment
When all things could fall in,

As indeed they may,
For all this peaceful scene, Boyne cease to flow
Broad through this green valley with
Its copious flood
Of ephemeral nature notes,

Such as one swaying sunheaded reed,
Such as a crow daubed on the ripple of
A black poplar, a thrusting ash
In its hedgeleap carrying
The long horizon on a twig, twice.

Distantly a horn, not Herne and his hounds but
Esquires at play, a near hill rolls gold
For some unearthly reason,
And maybe too this battered helmet of a place
I straddle cold

With sheep suddenly on the fosse;
Souls? No, merely ewes
And wearing the ram's pigments, the autumn's raddle;
Fertility minds its own business;
And world will go on more or less

The same notwithstanding God
Or Goddess; only man the danger. Still
It must be heartening in ill times to have
Ties with the whole network,
God on the wire inside a hill.

Jaguars roll from the meet, trailing
Horseheads and dogfoxes. History
Is slowly reaching some conclusion somewhere;
And here is the usual tentative dusk
As day runs out of silver

And one flintnebbed swan owns all the Boyne;
No afterglow or
Gold bowl to sail home the antlered one,
Surrogate, heraldic sufferer,
Cernunnos, Arthur, Bran.

Kiltartan Legend

Penelope pulls home
Rogue-lord, artist, world wanderer,
Simply by sitting in a house,
Its sturdy genius;
Of all sirens the most dangerous.

She'll sit them out,
The curious wonders, the ventriloquial voices,
Spacious landfalls, the women, beds in the blue;
Her oceanography
The garden pond, her compass a knitting needle.

The arc-lamped earth, she knows,
Will burn away and she
Still potter among her flowers waiting for him;
Apollo runs before
Touching the blossoms, her unborn sons.

Knitting, unknitting at the half-heard
Music of her tapestry, afraid
Of the sunburned body, the organs, the red beard
Of the unshipped mighty male
Home from the fairy tale;

Providing for him
All that's left of her she ties and knots
Threads everywhere; the luminous house
Must hold and will
Her trying warlord home.

Will she know him?
Dignity begs the question that must follow.
She bends to the web where her lord's face
Glitters but has no fellow
And humbly, or most royally, adds her own.

Yeats at Athenry Perhaps

1

We had our towers too, a large
Stone soldiery at bridge and gateway, they
Were the whole town once;
And I could have nodded to him from the top
Tendril of ivy or a jackdaw's nest;
But I'd never heard of him, the famous poet
Who lived as the crow flies fifteen miles away.

Certainly he'd have touched us changing trains
For Gort, have hours to idle, shared
The silence of our small town shell;
Maybe he passed me by
In a narrow-gutted street, an aimless
Straying gentleman, and I
The jerseyed fellow driving out the cows.

Ours was a sightseeing place that had
Exhausted history, but old wars had left
A dead king and a moat
And walls still half alive that watched
From towers with broken rims. I doubt
He bothered with us, all his sight turned in;
Some poems come better waiting for a train.

And that winged footprint could have jarred
The peasant metres of a street given over
To baker, grocer, butcher and
The treadmill of the till. What would he think
Of our outcropping sheds, the architecture
Of the very necessary animal?
And little better our weathered Famine chapel?

But on the eve of May he might have found
Things near his heart, Fertilities
Dropping in;
For then from consecrated ground we moved
The Virgin to the leafing trees
With bonfires, chanting children, the whole works;
The Canon hadn't read the latest books
On golden boughs and odd divinities.

Or would he have looked superior, been difficult
About Our Lady's face, the soft Italian
Look of the milking mother, not the sort
That strings the whole air like a catapult?
This was no moon in women, no
Unpredictable lady sailing
Her wavy shell;
Ours kept the house and answered the chapel bell.

Or so we thought or didn't think at all.
Diana has her secrets from the oak;
The nunlike night commits itself in strokes
Of barbarous shorthand when the candles die.
What's fifteen miles? We could have read together
The same nightscript, felt the vibrations run,
Boughs singing, with the whole south moving up
To stand in a dripping arch of spring.

I'd like to think how over the sheep and crops,
The nut-creggs and the loose stone walls we met
In a mutual hazard of burning arrows, but
I was too small then, my wavelengths caught
In anything low-down as a hawthorn tree
And jammed there for a day or all the summer,
Time no object, profession poetry.

Anyway he wouldn't have dared a town
Where every peeling window was an eye;
We smiled of course at strangers, proud
Of a dead king, the lordly
Dung that simmered in the ground. But I could
Have walked him round the moat, in Kingsland shown the rock
Where the crown toppled from the last Irish head
And a royal footsole left a bloody track.

No, he'd have sat down by the line and waited
Melting his bits of ore or watched the sky
Jolt from the saltmills of the Atlantic over
A town that died so often of the rain;
Why muddy a feathered foot when a great house waited
Over in Coole among the trees
(He liked his heraldry alive, well baited)
With all the amenities for Muse and man
Leda's kingbird on a lake, a lawn
For Juno's peacock, tranquil as a frieze.

Stop on the Road to Ballylee

I read Horace here
Where the lunatics now shamble around
The wrong side of their shadows. Kore or the moon
Have no pity. Mouthfuls of air,
Said the Big Tower, that's what we are.

Q. Horatii Flacci Carminum Liber 1;
Elementary classics, small blue book, Macmillan.
Our soft Cs were true Italian.
                              These
Overlay the place, shamblers
Stuck with the upper air,

Illustrating something, limbo or something, not
Like Liber 1 with its fauns and coins, Spring
(After a Pompeian wall painting;
At the woman's unsubtle nipple the first lamb yawns)
As if they saw behind the scenes

Not the Discus Thrower, page 9 –
From a marble in the Palazzo Lancelotti –
Never that, no more, or the Greek boy with the jaculus, my own
Age, page 10;
                  I tossed it too but antiquity magnifies.
Inward or outward these eyes?

Eight of us that drank the air here.
Now joy is difficult (like Beauty), but the big tower would have us
Make our verse like his, sing
Jubilant Muses. And these sad quidnuncs
Sidling by and round some broken thing,

Avoiding commitment; some woman laid them
Low or they denied her, Mater Saeva
Cupidinum – what ode?
                      Some fellows sacked for her, plucked
                                      burning
After lights out from the sidereal bush
(In the haggard with a skivvy, in the hay)

Flagrante dilecto behind the fawnstoned ballalley
And sacked. What end to those fellows?
The bogmaidens walked away with some fine scalps.
(For the matter in an ode, to penetrate to
The great beat, thrown out, lost extra muros.)

And these are husked, the flail is on them, unbuttoned
The only seamless garment, it is the dinginess
Hurts, affronts.
And Hermes (curvae lyrare parens) fashioning the toy
For love and the echoes of, for resonance;

Lynx lion tree-stumped, flamingo
Grounded by that lute, and the hells too in suspension,
Held up by a lover, Orpheus page 13
Where the dead hung off like these from the barbarous new ghost
With all that sounding metaphor, like these, the lost

Who still drift in the old flesh, confusing the
Gods, who no longer sing to their own wires
Or hang together
In the beat that is one beat, the all-beat.
Eight we were in the fine young weather;

Bright flashes, and some gone down Earth's
Hollow foundations.
                              (That other Hermes, the conductor, what
Page, psychopompus, with a soul for Charon's fishprow.)
Time to go now, time to be on the way.
(That was a woman the winghatted God had in tow)

Reminding me of that old girl being led away
Half dead at the top and too much down below.
Graveclothes the heavy skirts she heaped up to her navel,
The raw focus of it, and they bundled her away,
Poor soul not down yet to the ultra violet ghost,

In the main Asylum grounds O years ago
                              Edited by T.E. Page,
A prig but he did leave Faunus that field artillery.
Something came through,
A name, a coin, a winged horse,
Inked over by yours truly where they walk now,

The unburied
Illustrating something, Limbo or something, the unregarded
Who underlie us.
               Three measures
Of clay and we're at liberty to leave
To lay our tin wreaths on more iambic matter
At the Big Tower (those centenaries!)
In Ballylee, Ballylee,
Through Loughrea and Kilchreest where my own kin lie strewn
In the all mothering weathering Galways skies,
To a dead swan in Leda's thighs.

On the Tower Stairs

1

Arrow slits with heads
Of bitter weather; even here on this
Stone spindle winding up I have to think of her,
A dugout deity, a disconcerting
Earth mother living on.

Outwardly just a plain
Dump of a woman; no planetary body this
To magnify or disintegrate, genius
To no man. Yet Symons
All crow and ominous had sensed the siren

That afternoon she'd dropped in at Tulyra
Where he and Yeats were summering. 'La Strega',
Quoth the Temple Beau sniffing
The quite ordinary meat –
Which makes no witch of her and no carnivorate.

Nor a Beardsley black and white
Alive with insomnia in
Her widowed woods and swanlake. This was a lady
Given to no love
But a house and the glory thereof;

Stumping her walks for boundary and trespass;
And there was a diary
Voluminous, with the low trajectory
Of the Galway grass; and there was this
(Mr Gregory's Postbag) biography

Of a long-gone dismal hack who'd dined
On the Castle periphery, another of the husband-father
Who from a simple
Bible household bare
As a tent translated her

To rooms where books
Were accepted inhabitants. He'd held the gorgeous
East in fee, somewhere a governor
Before her time –
Ceylon, I think, where the tea comes from

And elephants dance round Buddha's tooth.
Take it easy, this
Is a serious lady ready for a new
Dispensation. Did she know it
Watching him, the gangling poet

In square, or is it trine, with Martyn's woods
Which rumour had it he was rocking
Some nights with lunar incantations?
What did she see
Beyond the too obvious anarchy,

Locust buzz and face of honey? The prophet authentic,
Like Midsummer John all lovely head?
Divining in
The endless budding of the wand
A lord of wine?

What were her chances?
A man with an arrow in his heart and a lifetime woman
More turbulent than a Muse;
And she with her cruse of oil half spent, in
The crepuscular shiver of the menopause?

A dumpy vernacular Victoria
Ruminating homewards to her moated bed,
(The very road I took this morning
In the downpour)
How did she manage it, capture the speaking head?

Maud Gonne from her hawklegged heights at eighty laughing
(Never in this tower she, never
On this stair)
'She did try to play Kathleen… but
She lisped so badly, poor dear.'

Vanity? (That bronze
In Charlemont House?) What does it matter now?
Who can question the work done?
I stand in the rainblitzed light
Outside, in the dogstare of the door.

Her trumpeted house is gone, entirely razed;
But he did raise up another
There on the totem pole in which the lady is
Oracular and quite composed
To outlast everything, live on forever.

The Small Town of John Coan

1

Invent them for us,
The open storeys overhead: we need
Them, the overplus, the changing
Bodies and a new seed.

Let Olympus overhang the street
And gossips will be poets. I want to see.
Cornuted bulls, and amorous
Birds in the family tree.

Strict biology
Caters to no truth we need. Who hid
In Juno's robes
Begat a god

And time and things like towns
That burned famously and battles that would yield
Hubbub and talk enough
For any man in a field:

Give us the lady's name
Who hides in the golden shower; boredom
Is where we lie now, with never a window
On Messalina's Rome;

And the sad river never
Manages to be Cydnus, never will float
Even in dream pharaoh's
Daughter or gilded boat.

Amoris domina, saddle this
Golden ass to break through to the tale
Of new dimensions;
Mother of love, command another Fall,

New Eve, new Adam, a new tree,
Gardens where nymphs are
Stories of air and water; let there be
Pipes in the air,

The cobble break
Into the blue, the town tumble into apple
Blossom, the Graces nude and linked
Lead out the season in a dancing rabble.

2

And just when he was all in it,
From head to foot the welling heartbeat,
This thing, this town, ceased to articulate for him.
Some ogre behind the font?
Some field god tired of making wheat?

Shocked when a child sister
Was walked in her deadbox to the old church
He saw the light turn sinister:

Some one had moved the morning
With an almost invisible lurch
And set it down askew.

Afterwards certainly all world was
Out of the true
Morning after morning.

3

Semele's son
Squandered to the riot buds in a field,
His privates blown, a no-man
Dowsed and spelled:

The unplotted torso swells; in the round
Of the year he rolls, reason enough for those
Revolving set-pieces; and in demand,
Season burgeoning from season; every woman his.

Autre temps,
    What so eager happens now?
What neighbour hill is begging me to die,
Offering endless resurrections?

Now spring is harnessed to a commonplace,
What rose glows in Cancer? What boy's face
In the empty stubble can autumn contemplate?

4

The portrait of Mrs O
Overall is black with
One eye bead sunken in
A beaked shawl.

The eye's the thing, receiver of
Dismembered cities if needs be. There
The Town is
Upside down in the harsh indifferent glare.

She broods in sombre areas; pruned
To crucifixion are the trees in her garden;
She stands on all the ways out in some

Survival like rock, won't go
Into water colours ever; simply shares
Her matter with some old-fashioned status quo.

The Christmas Vigil

Wherever else the real miracle
Was happening, with climates curtsying
To the small holy city, out here
On the west periphery
Our Galway weather hadn't nodded east.

Elsewhere the nub
And circles of rejoicing heaven, stars high and low
Lifting to the skyline
The figures of donkey, man and virgin
Moving towards Bethlehem.

So, on the old cart
Bumping on the road by Lopdells, today
Had not arrived, the trees
With aboriginal arms still making
Yesterday's rain

From the day's soft grey substance; no
New magnitude in the stone
Fields, no distances starting to flow
Into rainbows; there was only this
Same old world with yesterday's leftovers.

All the way to Mountbawn, with
Bullocks in a horned frieze staring
Egyptian from the roughmasoned gateways, ours
Storming the cart as we appeared;
We tossed them their turnips and went wheeling

Over the usual earth. Obviously
Christmas had not come to the brutes on this
Waterhaunted ledge of the Atlantic. It
Was quiet in the lambing paddocks, the ewes
Waiting at the troughs

In sops of gold straw for the broken oats;
And we dished it out, we two
Shepherds of sorts though no sky would open
For Nicholas Moran pipe in mouth now
And quite happy in his wingless span

Of Galway clay. Me too, for miracles belong
Over the ultimate horizon; nothing here
Has learned the rudiments,
No beast of ours
Drizzling over his fat roots will turn celestial,

Unlike the Bible ox
In the crib under the organ gallery, where
With a star strung like a kite above
And the new lunation in its eye,
The beast lights up with human love.

But this is the mystery welling
Up from some inner world in a sort
Of perennial heartbeat. All day the glow of it
Fills the back of my mind; but I won't look;
Not yet

Being simply afraid of what could happen.
I like things as they are,
World as it is, the wonder just round the corner;
And if at midnight
All the clocks in the world meet to chime

Over the world's newest child, this
Will be the more spacious for happening in my sleep
Where ends can meet in peace
When the great harps sweep out upon the pediments
And the wren waken with a tiny cheep.

Coat of Arms

On Sundays the marvel
Was there early, like
A white stag in the grazing. Up the long
Lane to the belfry we children hung
On the feet of an old Mass-going man;
And it was making;
It was our turn to be looked upon

As if for once we
Had some distinction, the fields unyoked and
Turned loose, all occupation gone
But the business of man
In the holy city
That had no spires
Visible or choirs, a faint angelic land.

Nevertheless we
Stand there in a tree of neighbours,
Our feet in the
Broken artery of a bog village
Till the bell summoned us
To the other side of
The walled world that could be ours.

And I am already afraid
And suffering a mystery
That turns cold the faces the summer sun
Edges gold;
The strong are down upon their knees,
The ogham heads are
Bowed to the happenings on an altar stone.

Heraldic the
Manwoman who
Feeds the fire there, dilating into
Hands that lift, bless, flow:
We belong to a journey into air;
Bell and gong
Announce our presences elsewhere.

Come back.
I sweat it at the side
Of Sunday man, feeling the static shake
In a tide of invocations. Now Monday seems
Most kindly for its implements
And farm animals, all men
At home in the homely house of flesh

Drudging in stone fields
Or high on the creeled cart marketing.
Miracle is
The priest's portion
And the Latin
That came down the muletrack where Hannibal
Stalled with his elephants.

It ends;
Missa est, and
What was to be accomplished is done;
Deflates with the harmonium;
But not quite, for out there
Hanging in the blue or
Alighted in the unyoked fields is a Sunday air

Mild and
Antlered in trees, that follows
And retreats, that will neighbour us
All day, our playfellow
And almost come to hand;
And begone by tomorrow when
Monday takes over the land.

Magna Mater

A dove plus an
Assenting virgin is
An odd equation; the bird of Venus, the
Shotsilk woodhaunter and
A country shawl
In congress to produce
The least erotic of the gods.

Afoot on Sunday, walking green
The little roads or high
In the spring carts, they come to Mass;
Hundreds who know man,
For whom no string was plucked
Or any heavens
Thrown open;

No dichotomy
Affects the prayer; that heaven
Should have one love, and earth another seems
Entirely natural.
What Troubadour
Built this country chapel?

And out of what
Substance? Harping on what nerves?
Mothers here
All virgin, fathers none,
The child a gift of heaven
And held in common by
Each virgin mother.

O indestructible
Country mulch the Muses tread
So delicately, into the earth you go
Breeding, tending
Where flowers are born with the names of kings
You never heard of, pagan fellows
Whose histories and business
Are open secrets in your
Sunshining faces.

For Paddy Mac

Once, so long ago,
You used to probe me gently for the lost
Country, sensing somehow in my airs
The vivid longlipped peasantry of
Last century

And those bronze men pushed
With their diminishing herds far out on
The last ledge of original earth,
Fomorian types
In the big one-eyed sky

All messed up with sundogs and
Too many rainbows, and that wishwashing head of Bran
In the toppling arches seaward sailing and singing
On his weathered maypole from
A caved-in skull.

Ours were the metres
Of early waters, the first argosy hardly home
With new women, orgies
When the moon rode round
Stone circles counting her twelve.

Homer's people,
And wasn't I lucky, born with
Boundaries floating, language still making
Out of the broadlands where my fathers
Tended their clouds of ewes?

Bunkum, Dear P. The thing was gone, or
Never was. And we were the leftovers,
Lord-ridden and pulpit-thumped for all our wild
Cudgels of Gaelic. Ours was Lever's
One-horse country; the bailiff at the bighouse door.

And hags hung all day
In turfsmoke among the fowl where I was licked.
That was a town
Walled and towered as Troy, and never sieged for a woman:
Trading bullocks and pennies for glory gone;

And watched from the top of a shilling the homespun fellows
Selling their spades on hiring days,
For a year and a day the dear flesh off their bones
From penury to slavery,
The soul thrown in for a spare.

That was my country, beast, sky, and anger:
For music a mad piper in the mud;
No poets I knew of, or they mouthed each other's words;
Such low-powered gods
They died, as they were born, in byres.

Oh, maybe some rags and tatters did sing.
But poetry, for all your talk, is never that simple,
Coming out of a stone ditch in the broadlands
Newborn, or from
The fitful pibroch of a lonely thorn,

Or old saws at winter fires.
Muted the big words. Love was left
To eloping earls or such
Lest the snake creep up, usurping the ancient timber
And some odd bloom come bursting from the Cross.

2

And you speak of Raftery, that bold tongue, the tramp
In borrowed bootleather, those rainy eyes
Lifted to empty heaven from a blind man's stick;
I sang like him you say, and praised women,
And I had the true cow's lick;

You who should know how every poet must
Baptize first the font and the very waters,
And have no godfathers but this great thirst
For what is not;
And no mothers;

Who must quote Ambrose crookedly (Nam quid divinus
Isto ut puncto exiguo culpa cadet
Populi), bog Latin for
The bit of earth we tread
Into metaphor.

Knowing we're just another civilisation
To be dumped, but go on, say it you,
We've eaten all the gods yet bow the knee,
And are only really at home
In the larger toleration of the poem.

Carefully, now that you are dead,
I must amend the scribbles of the tribe
Lest sheepman and bullhead
Become a frieze of fathers like stone man,
Hieratic, almost Egyptian,

And from the uncreated, with arms widespread,
From puncto exiguo, beyond the dead
And Lazarus rising, where God is making still
Release the flood
Of living images for good and ill.

Dear P. I'll never know
What you brought over and passed on,
But this seems certain as I grow:
Man lives; Gods die:
It is only the genuflection that survives.

Lost Man

In an old green book, mouldering
From the window ledge, sitting under
A lamp globe made in Bohemia,
I read once how to grow turnips;

In a tiny thatched house where a ladder
Cocked up to a loft above the kitchen,
Simple as the first working skeleton,
Warm as the breastwork of a pigeon;

With a cobbled yard to the little local road
That was kitchen too with a sky roof,
Ruled by an old matriarch who still spun wool
On a wheel of bog oak:

Byres, carthouses, turfricks, pigsties,
The place was open as a bird's nest
To the weather, the fields, the planetary animals,
The sun had his corner like another beast.

Neighbours too, nodding in, or high
On a creeled cart, mobile in a geography
That never moved till Sunday
Were names, roots, lineage, graphs and grafts of the one tree,

Our gossips, our daily dialogue; in
An odd way too the faces of their fields
Showed through them, the tilt of thatch or turfrick
An aura about them, their identities.

So reading by the bright wick, with
A large moth tapping out the vague
Morse of a summer's night
And the old lady at her steady wheel

Earth rolled small enough to
Be caught in the heartbeat. It was small
As I and manageable, spun to no savage foot;
And my need was to be rooted in the soil

I knew, with a village for a capital,
A spire on Sunday where a local God
Woke up to find some majesty above
The weather or the weekday sod

Where in his working clothes, in grace and grain
And grass he forgot his cherubim and trumpets,
Walked boundaries, was amenable to ewes
And quiet moonbodies like fat turnips.

Mine, of course, was a crop that never grew,
Or could be grown,
Being a life where an old girl used a wheel
Of bog oak, adze-hewn

And sand-honed by a country master long
Before the making of her world
Who laboured by diplight or hearth's glow
Till the thing worked.

Special for Nancy's Mother

Gentle lads, I know
Big moments are
Bodies with heartbeats, outlasting
Sun, moon and star;

That hill-struck with
The sheepmen, high
The weather perches on your looks,
The mountain stares you squarely in the eye;

And is yours, all
The youth and the big views of
Small boys become soul
And love

Where, up here and forever,
Boys you are,
Bodies of place and moments
You scarcely remember

Which are your life now and
Illumination;
Death being merely
Life's big double, the larger twin,

And you still happen,
Wake with morning on
The top pastures, push
The boat into the sun,

Are two brothers with a sister, are
Scree and sky
Between the two waters,
Are all the eye

Ever beheld or the heart felt;
Day never done,
Night still a golden place
With a sleeping sun.

So, dear boys, having all
The footprints, welcome
A new brother, where
Forever you are at home;

And show him
Gravely around yourselves, with
The grand manner of natural powers, like
Weather or myth,

Who stands gravely too
At your threshold, waiting
The almost visible smile,
Your almost visible greeting.

Brigid her Eve

for Nancy and Conor and a rush Cross

Origins are
Swamps and rush cradles, so never
Mind me if I see
You as no lady but barbarous and
Maybe beautiful, as when
The scurf of winter grass in Galway
Ignites to light or
Rain and you are nothing less
Than metaphor

That I do not care to
Resolve ever and won't ever bother to
Catch close and make small like
Another woman or even
A tower of ivory or house of gold, thus
Missing out on major things like weather
And distances that touch
Other distances right round this
Only and mighty orb.

I know the feel of
Up through my legs since
I staggered erect from the
Tremors of trees, in which you
Were a bark skirt and a
Dogbite of roses, most fecund for
A boy lover. And you, do not
Come closer either, for there is
Nothing nearer.

Just simply be;
Continuing, with my own bit
Of history evaporating while
I find big things in consonants, like the
Discovery of a spring well, or
The hunch of a spring plough on the first headland
When all the world was a vowel;
Big things like lost continents;
Something that has your style.

Or lack of style,
Like the raw bulb of the ewe that leaves
A lamb on the green, or the
Tiny earthquake of a snowdrop, nothing
To shake the poles too much, just something
To show you've been around and the day holy
Like Sunday or lucky like
The day when a poet is lucky enough to say
Something of importance to himself

That must
Acknowledge and ignore you, the miracle
Taken for granted, being natural,
As the fields turn over, China
Falling as we come up,
And I stand flatfooted on a slanting land
Content with the old lore, with the womb language
That built you with the sun in a rush
Cross to be hung on every door.

Lost Man in Me

1

He can forgive
Enormous sins with ease; Hitler at his ear
With the drums of delirium
Not too hard to bear;

Nor the little men that sell out
Neighbour and passion. Inside his tree
Equating leaf and trunk
The big is no more than the moiety,

And the hugest trulls beam
The shy lamps of virgins; on the Petrine rock
The worst popes shine like artifacts;
Not theirs the shepherd's crook

But his for who knows
Who corrupted whom? Not he who stares
At Messalina in the Roman whorehouse
And wholly admires the wares;

And is not too put out when Catherine
Garrots her man. Behind his fan
He listens to Lesbos singing and the voice
Sweet as duet and duel says all that love can:

Which is neither more nor less
Than you, me, sun and moon. He quotes the Hai Ta'u –
'The supreme virtue of heaven is to produce';
And leaves it to me and you,

As if our generals were mere gun
Barrels to a moment that waits upon the trigger.
If any unpin the bomb,
It's in the Thing itself and will it matter?

A round of Yin, then
A round of Yang, that equals the Tao. In
His tree already he forgives them, if
Forgiveness is possible without sin,

As if all
Were turning sweetly on the potter's wheel, the gross
Fungus and the girl about to fall.
The virtue of heaven is simply to produce

Anything. It's a music. Birdsong or bomb
It's all equal. In his Yin-Yang tree
He doesn't ape God but is quite like some
Kind of eternity

In whose paradox I can sing
Who sits in my tree
A million-million years doing nothing
But forgiving me.

Down there, mast high,
He hangs above the world's waters;
Inch after inch he clambers into the sky
On a wincing rope.
This might be the day to die.

One hand holds, one desperate claw
Battered sea-black, green and blue.
The other tears at the canvas gale;
Lurching on a seatop he
Empties the belly of a sail.

Seabooted, unwieldy, wearing no
Wings he should be foundering down
Latitudes that turn to snow;
Instead, he spins
The rough earth on the axis of one toe.

And with a single ropeyarn he
Tugs the hugely blackening west.
The compass in his head is true;
All points at rest.
His bird is married to the sea.

This could be the day. He rolls
Surgewise, seeking it. The shiver
Of water piles up to the Pole.
He jumps the first backstay down,
Spits in a fist, sails on forever.

Lakshmi

A sheet of paper, placed
Over this dangerous bronze figure,
Covers up the East
And the dancer's narrow waist,

India gone, sunken
The archaic shining knot; white paper
Is the churned-up ocean
That casts her upwards, buttocks in motion,

Helmeted hair, enormous
Ear-rings and all, the necklace
In sacred circles; there was
Dancing here that folded into a lotus.

The bare breasts still now, the nubs
At rest, but the twisted rhombs
Of the hips still echo
Temple gongs.

The belly is so young
And the undented navel. Instruments
Should sound like this,
Keeping distance

Like the long arm that falls to the gathering fingers,
Hand sinister, that knows space
Is precious and must not spill.
The two legs are tough with grace –

And since they are the bearers, yield nothing
To immodest silks, who must tower
Up from their native earth
To carry a little flower

Where, coppered above
The heartbeat, on its fine meridian floats
A face flawed with neither age or youth;
Here Ganges pours

But merely rounds the bud
She contemplates, that must not dwindle;
On her right hand it rides, and earth
Turns quietly on the spindle.

Three Houses

1 *Gurteen*

I had no gift for it.
It hung out in the welter of the moor;
A black-faced country staring in

All day. Never did the sun
Explode with flowers in the dark vases
Of the windows. The fall was wrong

And there was uplifted the striking north
Before the door.
We lived in the flintlights of a cavern floor.

It was enemy country too, the rafts of the low
Fields foundering. Every day the latch
Lifted to some catastrophe, such as

A foal dead in an outfield, a calf lost
In a mud-suck, a hen laying wild in the rushes,
A bullock strayed, a goose gone with the fox;

The epic, if any, going on too long.
Nil the glory in it, null the profit;
It was too big for me and full of threat.

A place that glugged green in the vast egg
Of the weather, too littered with rains
And with minor stone-age tragedies like getting wet

Feet in the goose paddock watching
An angel, yes, in the air, in the dusk, taking
A rose petal face out of nothing in particular,

Just happening big out of a glitter,
Unaware of me or the black-avised country where
The half-wheel of the day was bogging down.

Certainly it could have been the moon.
And though I prefer to think otherwise
Nothing happened in the way of ecstasy.

And I took indoors my gawky childhood, still
Unmeasured, through mud and the yard midden
That was acting up and coming into the kitchen

With the milkers, with the men, with the weather,
Feeling as ever that the earth is outside matter
Trying to get in, to get into the very centre,

Swamp the sunflowers and stone circles
And all that spirals and wings up, to bring
The tiller back on the old compost heap,

Dung value. Petering out
Like this father-figure at the fire
Crumbling into space, who was something once,

Who was the sage here and the reason, who raised
The roof, begot the tree,
Hedged the apple and built the causeway down

For the postman who never comes, who touched
The harsh sex of the earth that never blooms,
And was gentled by this woman who stands in the door now,

The mistress of a few iron pots,
With the bogface looking in and the barbarous furrows.
I tell of my angel and the bright thing is lost

In the cud of cows, in the farming day,
Never to bloom again and wash the air
Towards Clonkeen Carle. I sit down by the fire

And build my nightly stockade in the ash
With an old catalogue, Army & Navy Stores,
And polish two pennies bright

While earth and day go under. Buoyed up
In their bundles on the nightwave are the plovers,
Blown with the sweet pith of their bones over, the men

Drift off to visit other outposts of
Man in nameless townlands, moon-swollen damps.
The two old people sit it out,

And humped in the very posture of the womb
On a small stool I ride it too,
The dull incessant siege, on the black orb –
The epic, if any, going on too long.

2 *Shanballard*

It's feeling now and dangerous
To touch, when I
Was the crown prince of birds early
With the first cock crowing;
And that was a morning,
My head pillowed and abroad
In the true blue;
Meaning I felt the world awake
And I was a county.

Meaning up heartwise the house awoke
To the call of a country;
Turfsmoke curled from below
And day creaked open;
Dangling on my rafter I
Survey my kingdom,
Open fire and hanging kettle,
The doorway wide,
The feathered collie in the morning beam.

Meaning the big unsteady dawn was waiting
And world still making,
Meaning the smoking cows halfmade
Wavered on the dews;
And there was a snail humped on a bridge
And there was the blackbird pecked him up
And there was the mare I was to ride
Butting a silly liquid foal.
The day was starting to report.

Meaning it zigzagged off the arrow
Head of a woodcock, meaning it caught crows
Burgling a turnip field, meaning it sat
On the old crowman in the oats,
His crossbow more askew;
Green hung the crabapple claws;
Rabbits announced me, here
Comes Twolegs and his totem dog;
The thumped morse went on before me.

Meaning it went up into the breath
Of morning, meaning I bowed before
The bowlegged blackthorn in the gap
Where the sunburst met me.
And I was the bogvoice going up,
I was the beginning bees,
I was the dialogue in the curlew's mouth
And simple as a two-holed pipe;
The ripe fern turning south.

Meaning the sun was sailing me, and all
The call of crows on Lynch's knoll was mine;
And lying down I was
The newest butterfly white and green
Drying its wayward compass on a stone,
And the all around and the all to be
Turning over
To catch the three small chimneys on the hill
Treadling the morning smoke.

Meaning the cat loped after the milker
And swallows chuckled
On the byre beams above the cans, meaning
Pigs sang at the sty gate,
And two old men,
Two lovely raggedly old men gossiped
By the upheeled cart, and morning
Was over, done, gone, and never
To be followed after;

Meaning I,
Catching the sun upon a breakfast knife,
No longer beamed;
Housed I was and never homed again,
A dwindled fellow.
Folded the buzzing miles outside the pane
Where the drunken gatepost leaned
And a single foxglove rolled its bells around
A stick tall as an umbrella.

3 *Knockroe*

The river god sat down
In Summer pools. The Satyrs or their male
Correlatives in Gaelic haunted
Bankside and haycock:
It was that season of the year.

Even the sun searched for the female form.
The dayscreen was hers, night flitted
As if from a halfmoon before her;
Her dayshift over,
She lived upon the scandals of the night.

I was the wooded brute then on the road,
Horns in the night bush. Unlimited
The fight, the free-for-all; no
Woman could cover that
Amount of country, so the country did it,

And blocked her out in capitals of trees
On hills and tapped the air
For delicate lights, as I for words. It went
Hard with me
In the old Landleaguer's house,

Dowsing the summer's water, raking hay,
Handling a horse or footing next winter's turf
Yet it went gay with me who thought
She must be there, be here,
Would come, would come, all things being right,

Who heard the old men talk, the old men say
Something that belonged to her and me,
Land war or cattle stir, some small
Epic with a lift
Was a tall heroic body we could share,

Shining, one to the other, two top
People with a need for deeds. I trained
Tough for something that would never happen,
But happened daily
And ever would happen, being simply me.

Come you now and take the words that make you,
Oblivious twin, all woman, my one peer;
My dark, my darling, full of rage and grace,
Come, Goddess,
Of all your faces show me just one face.

Sunday Morning

If I make way for bells on Sunday morning,
Demure, deep in
Her Sunday hat she'll walk, tipping the tall
Flowering shrub, a lilac, at
The corner
Turning into Mespil Road.

A street new from the font, an old
Arrow of canal
Mounted, tufted by an ancient swan, is leading
Somewhere;
My bible woman hardly knows
The way she goes.

She carries the total injury of me;
In jeopardy. Almost
Rural the scene with elm and planetree, sun
At summer hoist, a wisp
Of smoke from some pedestrian;
Her penitent feet will lead her on.

She does not dally by the sluice
Or the resting barge. An odd head
Hangs on the bridge at Baggot Street;
God is dead,
His shadow what I throw for
Beyond into hurt and metaphor.

The whole world can see the lover's hands
Upon her. In the din
Of sweet bells she rises to confess
The evil bruise;
Hears another gospel start
In the regions of the heart;

What penitence can she profess?
How burn away
Back into her first
Girl-smile
The garden fallen around her, simple trees,
Lovers and enemies?

Trevaylor

First, this
Prayer, that you the people
Gone over, ghosts, bright
Narcissi, lean into my pool now
And be this poem.

Empty are
All mirrors you do not countenance;
The fabulous water is
Fathomed by no horizons
Till you come, till you appear.

I offer you
Only the barest stems. Sunflowers,
Come! Gather your lives
About me here. People
Me in those local airs

Which were yours, which
Are you, which
I breathe. Your flaws over me.
Let them rise and ruffle,
The colours rich

So that I have
Dimensions beyond me, where
You are form and dimension. Tread my
Mirror hugely, people,
That the great thing appear.

Painting of My Father

1

I saw him to the last, the grey
Casting of the face,
The crabbled hands like this
Yielding to the cluster of the Rosary;

I who barbered you occasionally
And filled your pipe
Dropping into your deafness the odd item
Of family news that never
Exactly reached you,

For you were away already.

So your true going was a sort
Of mutual release. 'Lord', you whispered hanging
That day in my arms naked
As Jesus down from the cross,
'Take me away'.

Now for me this vague distress
And a guilt that grows;
What is it that one owes a father?

And cannot pay,

Liaison lost with the broad
Dialect of the child where words
Were the throbs of a countryside

Big like a sheepshearing or small
As the lark pinned high above
The water meadows where we drank our tea,
The trout waiting in the fishing river;

Eternal precincts
Of a huge present tense, as if
You were not due to be left
Abandoned like an old
Settlement;
The young being
Unscrupulous in their growing up.

So you wanted little of me towards the end,
Barbering, a light
For the old pipe,
And an ear, my ear, any ear, when you spilled over
The intolerable burden
Of being a very old man.

2

An image that wounds;
Better even
The figure of power, the
All father,
Jahwah, Helios or another; not
That I'd like you in big translations
Who were rich enough
As your own man.

For you were daylight's own fellow and over
The moonsuck of the mother
All male and master under heaven;
And that's how you come into mind,
In taut middle-age when you were quite
The masher,
Velvet collar, tan velour
Overcoat, plush hat and handmade boot,
In those streets round the cattlemarket where
Our evenings were a summer saunter;

Hanlon's Corner, Stoneybatter,
The Broadstone, MGWR
Where trains run no more,

And I half expect round any corner
The hastening dandy, country
Things still clinging;
Blue the gaze;
Delicate the gait, the dancer,
Angler, fowler, hurler, football player;

Tomorrow
Formally as a bullfighter he'll pace
The horned pens and the cattle slobber,
Face the loss or net the profit
Stonily
As befits the gambler;

And at noon lean
Recomposed on the railed wall
By the City Arms, yarning, true Ulyssean,
Over a shoe shine.

3

And now here
Above the walnut desk, the only familiar in
This strange hallucinatory land I found
Late, you stare out; again
All age, all pain, at the very end
Of your long span: not you indeed
But every man;
Just waiting.

Land's End some few miles away; the tide
Is white round the mount; a bird
Stands on the sundial on the lawn; Spring
Is hovering;
And in the tulip tree – hallucination – some
Medieval person reads a tome

(To disappear battered
By a rainshower with his
Monkshood, creature of air;
The bird stays on, real enough;
A woodpecker)

A country ironed out
Into saints and menhirs where
You never put a foot,

Where the weather camps for an hour before
It stamps the soft shires, taking over
The whole south of England at a blow.

Curragh, November Meeting

Distances are
Threaded over, a web. And the same spider
Spins the tale of
The dying sun

Caught on his last legs. Bleaching too
Are the bright horses: jackets
And jockeys run
Out of pigment, are

A caveman's scratches, a jostling script.
There's some time left
To use your magic on it, wish
The winner home

Down Walsh's Hill into
The drumbeat of the straight. Here
We go offering
The thing a heart, the spectacle a home:

And half ashamed of it, the child's
Play, the toys in colour now
Thumping their own life out of us, galloping
Into the heart

And away. Gone. Tomorrow the
Empty stands, the moneyspinner in
His winter coat;
And all forgotten.
                          Nomads no more

It means nothing, nor should; a mock-up
Since we dropped that wild pulse settling down at last,
Suburban fathers: or at most a slight
Affair with a trumpet blast.

Athenry

1

The guidebook gives it date and dignity;
And disengages me. The place is alien.
Though I've rubbed raw against the geography
The heartbeat here's not mine;
Simply dead history.

Norman, it says, original walls; meaning
Those old stone wounds and moon mends,
Watch-towers gone native into
Treetops and birds' nests
Where I wished up the watching country

And purely civilian wagged with the daws
My early cradle, the warman
Dispersed among the thousand names of grass;
Honey is on the spike;
The golden skulls fall to the beekeeper.

I disown them, the masters and
The lordly Abbots greedy for heaven who holed up
Here in the very thigh of Christ,
I mean in the tumbled chancel where the East
Hangs crucified on one great Abbey window

And on a strut of stone I rode the beam
Of morning sometime I can't remember,
Ten townlands in my breath;
And truly a grassman with no history
Trod on every hill,

Rueveha, Raheen, Esker, Mountbawn, do
My footprints show
Where my fathers loom green into the blue
Hills of Roxborough?
How young I am in the plain of the bird's eye.

2

Notable for its cattle fairs, says the book
Follow me here. I am
The antlered boy,
A wood of horns my home. I move
Where great beasts in the street rise out of mud:

I go forth in a caul of dung. I
Am at home in the house of the people,
Their genuflections are mine,
Mine the Barbaroi with the green thumbs,
Cousins on the one dug.

Mark how this fair morning the very earth
Arrives on the doorstep, men
Who are wedges of weather, who will depart
On footprints of stubble, leaving
The dark down on the day

And a void that the mud fills, leaving
A mess; and as ever it's raining:
There's a cart abandoned at the town's end;
Casualties dribble in the pubs;
And my limping uncle's on the booze again;

I cry for the lift of the morning, whose clay feet
Are mud melting
Into that old drunk from Derrydonnel
Always the last and maudlin in the night
To home on his distant candlelight;

Ass-eared and tumbrilled, with his silent wife
He'll arrive; unlike me left
Wilting with the time, I
In the morse
Hoofbeats of the horse,

The jargon of the Gods maybe, and maybe
I tuned in on some heraldic thing:
(Erect me a monument of broken wings)
However divine the arguments
I lost them every one

And am so vulnerable I stand here now
At a town's edge shying
Away from some old misery. Quem tu, quem tu,
Melpomene… A fellow out of character
In any room but a field

Who wept at school, that whole first month,
For the great Inadequate left after
Where myth becomes fear,
Careful lest a living odour leak from the creature,
And the dog dig up Caesar.

The Small Town of John Coan (2)

1 *Remand*

Sailing the last date out and away
Beyond birthdays on face perhaps
May distract him from
Such infinities

As there are; a gaze,
Hardly a girl yet, pupped between two
Furloughs from Flanders Field;

She rose out of it with white paps
Aching so young they heaped his
Hands full.
                        What happened
To the doll face that brought to the half-doors
The town spinsters where on propped-up

Elbows they waited for time to round the tale,
Snake and apple fall?

2 *Maud Gonne*

In a Noh play she
Would be the heartbeat left
To some famous numinous name straddling
Haunted centuries of highway,

A passionate body caught
Between worlds in an endless jet
Of feeling, for whom the final death is not;

A silhouette
I keep seeking, remembering how an old
Shawled slum-body was transfigured on
The Metal Bridge one winter sunset

Walking out of the rose
Visored and greaved, in whole barbaric gold,
Bellona, War's own maiden, no simpering poet's Muse.

3 *Genius Loci*

Unthinking youth had sparked and fizzled to
The unceasing woman, yet never struck fire really
Till he was the sober pew, the settled piece
Of family furniture.
                          And then but the once
And only for a moment did earth roll back, the stone
Turn;
                          For a tinker Moll, absurdly garbed
In trailing handmedowns, in purple, on a ditch,
The tents behind her and all Tartary.

The conflagration was dowsed decently,
The bog road and the blue sat steady down,
Space filled up.

                          But there's a want
In every daylight since, a wayside place
Stretched to the limits with the savage face
Of the brute goddess its inhabitant.

4 *Encounter*

And I on the Alley Bridge
Unjointing the rod that evening, summer
Aloft and slow and
All the old ones out in Abbey Row

When behind me up she rears
In her daffodil jumper, her
Whoring number; and she peers into my fishbasket
Low, low.

Pisces two.
                          Some are dead
Who mumbled into her buttercups, gone down
The darling men, the King's very own.

And still it's on offer, that very ardent lap
Though it's said the battered elm in Leonard's lawn,
The lover's tree, has even got the clap.

Over the smother of the rain
His mother with a violin hung out of heaven;
La donna e mobile;

He answered her, spreadeagled on
The crutch of his own instrument, his face
In the buttend of a candle; rapt I suppose away.

That was in the bakehouse twenty years ago
When it was a melody –
              I mean Time
When it was his galleon, scrolled wind, hefted numen;
O Jesus what guttered on the puddle?
                  Dough in trow and bin
Waiting the morrow, the oven, the reality.

             He doesn't know
He'll leave too late, come back broken, sit
Over the trickling street on a sack of bran
With a foul pipe.
              No-man.

6

She'd thumbed her way from the source
Of every faery story, simply
Taking his over; a nudity
On a white horse.

At least that's what he'd like to tell;
Actually it fell
Out differently of course.

There was a horse all right, a fat pad
On which she
Our beauty rode

Spangled and pirouetting over the mud
And sawdust of Taylor's field, a circus ride.
He was aged six but that was the night
On which he was destroyed.

7

Sometimes I'd like to write: 'Dear Helen,
Admit me no more
Into the epic by
The back door.'

Like last night when I froze
In the yard with a barrel of rainwater,
A spy – I'd sunk that low –
On her new visitor.

Candle, glim, or blued lamp,
O great God in Heaven that
He should heap with light that ample rump
While the sky turned on my table and it grew late;

And she let him out where I coped with the night chills,
A freakish lad with wings on his heels.

Comment: when the bare
Triteness of age hums
With old Gospel words, when his deeds
Are nil and his needs nulled, ten to one she comes
Making a final last appearance;

        Never like this
In a fieldway holding
The heliograph of a daisy head.

    God
Be good to this lover. He watched her become
Too loud a music for the room
No matter the hand on the piano, his
Least of all in consequence,
    He earned his peace,
Breaking, being no glass to rise and fall
Intermittently to every squall.

He'll come back, stand exactly here –
Footprints never blow away like leaves –
Above him the same crows sawing;
It's spring always under the rampart trees.

He'll say: 'Time was when heaven loved a child'.
And for a simple moment that's what he believes;
And believes for a moment a world grown mild;

And perhaps pick up as before the same skyblue
Crow's egg unharmed and whole
From its tree fall.

Holding it the large unaching earth is true,
Forever the uttering birds, the leafy boy
Scored in the dapple, his small footprints
In the midst of great improbable events.

10

Clubbed by the evening bell
From the roughcast tower in goes the earlier man
To candle dip and soft shoes,
White surplice, black soutane.

He moves the holy place into the beam;
Now the westering south gives room
She rides in on a piece of glass,
A face more told than any tale.
                              The several
Pious souls inhabiting the aisle
Will never know his thurible is aimed
Beyond them, how maimed he is

Who watches the red wick in the colza oil;
Too mothered.
                              Always fronting him
Veronica holding out a towel.

11

He puts back on his severed head
And a town trite as a platitude
Offers him his face in blood;

And sings so sweetly with his mouth
The hurts of youth;

As if what lives – where suppurates
The history that has no dates –
Were bidding him lift up his head
Transfigured with neurotic dread

And listen to it giving tongue
Sweet as Solomon his song
For the young;

And all the sweeter for the art
Of the thorn in his heart.

12

Delicate
The sensual skin of our town; tap
A gable and the timbrel
Of a person answers;

Such a stuff, not stone, not timber,
Simply a state
Of being there, living the similar,
Or sharing a space

Or a common psyche, puffed large
Into the variable of the weather,
In which each one secretly
Seeks selfish some sodden glory.

But if one sins all fall. There's no assent
Yet the town twangs like an instrument.

Summer and a liquid bird
In the high stones: a tower
In a garden is something, like a sword
Upstairs.

But towers have lived so long
The gods have annexed them: in each a lover
Mailed and clinking yields to the dulcimer:
Mars is taken by a song.

Who mentioned Elenore?

A baker in a paper hat
Relieves himself against the rampart wall;
Over the privet blows an apple.

What would she dare
Here in the huge descending West? What troubadour
Would gild her scandals, offer her
Golden ball, golden sandals?

A Certain Person

Ten foot high is a lord;
Pallas Athene, give me
My portion now that I'm tired,
And a little man as a toady,

A certain plum-coloured codger,
And let him make me suit;
A little bum-wagging dodger
Of the third sex, and a tout;

One who's thrived on the flavour
Of lickspittle or worse,
An obscene jaunt whose saviour
Jingles in his purse;

A trull, a doll, a livery,
The smell of the Fall on his face;
A ludicrous little flunkey
Who stands between me and grace,

Stands ten foot high in his lord,
The money-changer; I say
I'm tired, lady, I'm tired,
For the traffic is all his way;

Osiris who weighs all souls
Sat poets high on a feather,
But this lout's fouled the controls
And we're back to the shoe leather;

He walks the town unloved,
Yet sits down everywhere,
A footboy once removed
Who's sneaked up stair by stair.

All I ask, Good Lady,
Is to pull off the ten-foot socks,
Sever the head from the body
And the jungle from the money box

And scatter the pieces fairly
Where they came from, where he crawls
Out in the scrawled graffiti
Of the moon in urinals.

Body

I'll wear it out perhaps
To a suit of wrinkle, a skin
Too large
With the soul shrinking;

The will gone out of it,
Yet all the daily rent to pay;
Flesh that cannot last,
Soul that never got under way:

Too much houseroom now;
Tomorrow none;
But paying either way
For journey done, for journey not begun.

A Bit of Brass

A horn hung on an oak;
And he, the big overplus, the hero
Destined, sounds the famous note, invokes
Cascading Gods and
His own death boat.

I did lift
A bit of battered brass once to my mouth,
May 1915, after
A day's rain
In the townwalled field where the Volunteers
Drilled;

That evening the wet overhang had daunted all,
Bugler and mate
Gossiped under a leaking branch, sounding
An occasional call,
Joe Egan, Josie Rooney;
Dear Posterity, I was there.

Echoes hung
Solidly in the drowned green beechtrees,
Hardly swinging;
Call after call brought no one to the field,
That is no man alive;
The mates gave up and I purloined the thing;

Squawk, a couple of fancy tootles,
Then out of Me minus
It came, the soaring
Thing;
Just once.

It could be it still hangs
In the May over
Leonards and the Pound Walk, just waiting
Those fellows, the long striders
Gods or men
To take the field.

Duddy's Wall

Mon semblable in
Tattered velvet, battered sandals, dangling
From his five years over
The goings on in Duddy's Livery Yard

Half morning has
Died on the sundial, the other half
Is the giant's eye on my forehead
Seeing everything

That happens, such as T. Heavey, Saddler,
Clambering over the Rampart wall to
Loosen his belt;
And a strawman in Shaughnessy's stack

Tilting at an old cow, eternal
Dragon of the gardens; and there's the Regan girl
Hobbled in red flannel pegging out
Her drawers:

Which facts I record, noting
At the same time how the rooks
Chuckle just outside my halo; world comes
Also over the treetops where the sky is

Moving in peaceful parables; not that
My geography goes round the sun, I am
The nub middle, sit, squat
On my stone butt surveying

One Mike Delaney, Ostler, in the echoes
Below me, talking guttersnipe
To a sad angled gearraun
Called Charley

Harnessing up, and a Duddy (Tommy) with
A barrow of new dung, both
Steaming, while Tom the Father
Beard and all comes following after

Leading another unarching bit of horseflesh
Fully caparisoned
For a funeral walk. Berny
Quinn is dead, poor man:

Clay pipes for every manjack mourner,
Snuff in saucers
For the weeping world on the kitchen board;
Already the bellringer's in the loft

And the family ghosts
Pleading for decent burial, reminding me –
Who digs the hole
For Berny Quinn, son of the carpenter?

Once I saw him topple in a fit.
Now this day is his, we follow him
Around two streets; proud heroes strut
For one perched high, tophatted, one Michael Delaney, mute.

(Who doesn't know as
He fly-flicks daintily one big gelding's ear,
How soon himself must go,
And how much further

Past the old tower undone
As a headless Knight, and into the fable
Of the fall-down Abbey.
Of a red haemorrhage on Duddy's table)

And that was a day in my fathering fellow,
First Adam, pre-fall,
Scuffing with a toe the planetary surface
On Duddy's wall.

The Skellig Way

The March crow furnishes his twig
In the knowledge that a bigger bird
Above the blow
Is hatching out the whole raw yolk of spring.

There's no Lent in the twitching rookery;
Pair by pair they go,
Feather to feather married;
Easter the nodal point in earth's revolution.

Listen, you dumb stone faces to the West,
You on Skellig Michael,
White hoods of God,
Hermits abounding in the unseen graces,

Matins, and Lauds and Vespers are sung here
In a loud vernacular
Above the trees;
Can you do better down on your knees?

Three Poems

1

Only here if
I look for them one sauntering forth
In her black shawl or
Pinned to the doorway with the long street
To one eye like a telescope;

The other just a face
Floating in the turnsmoke within;
She was the saint, hobnobbing with the greater galaxies,
Taking credit accordingly
When I passed examinations.

I love them now who never
Saw them really, or unwillingly: days
They look out of windy November with
The chimneys in a smudge
Of illiterate initials all down the street,

Alive, the darlings, in a sort of love for me;
Penury's hangovers, yet
How they'd hate this, to be the poor
Relations to a poem, tugged forth from
Their decent anonymity;

Bridget and Delia, spinsters deceased;
Tom brother, the breadwinner, carrying the can,
In the Temperance Hall the Parliamentarian,
And Michael the dandy with the highbred look of hunger
And the delicate impossible languor.

Too late I want to know them now,
Like God a lover, who must share with them forever
This furrow of a street
Full of the ghostly bloom
Of dead semen.

2

Beside them that lightfoot wife,
Stone barren,
Who drifted towards the hornmad in the way
The moon sinks
A well in every water drop.

And I wonder, outside charity, what image
Of love she begat in them
Who watched her, the Who's Who
Of town lovers,
Corrupting the nightwatch and the family rosary:

Barren naturally; then –
Hallucinated Jesus – to grow round as a plant pot
In the parlour window!
To shake it out, the blessed blossom, like
The very mother of God, in the chapel aisle,
Sunday's woman!

What invisible lover beaked her nape, to be
After forty years in fruit, adding
The unbearable mystery of fatherhood?

As if, in a chagrin of virgins, some new thing was mooting
Like a dispensation; Moses
Down from the barbarous rock-face, still
Shaking with rainbows.

3

I'd like to assure myself I really saw her
The new girl,
Walking down the street the first day,

And not borrowed her from the poet
Of another wobbly old town, that died
Three thousand years ago,

That offered to the summer evening a like
Paraphernalia, old men on the sills,
Iron ringing in a forge.

I cannot recollect if I was rolling a hoop
Or playing with the taus
When I heard the new silence and discovered her

Passing on the bare uncobbled way, leaving
An Iliad behind,
Just liberating the one line

That grows and grows into resonance, as if
She touched him in passing,
The old man of Chios, who was blind,

Who needed only the whisper of her sandal
To set the topless towers on fire,
Consuming incidentally all women else,

So that it hurts me to try to remember
How much I remember of a face that's disappeared
Nameless in the glory of another.

Yesterday's Man

I sit staring
At the old notebook. And that was the year
That never, I thought, rose off the ground,
The dull one, nose to the grindstone,
Unabashed by lack of wing:

Yet here, confronting me
With an air of great doings, is an old familiar
Still edged and luminous with
Its ache towards infinity, striving
Out of the very mortality of my parts

To strike the attitudes of (circa) 1480
Pico, Ficino, of Florence, Platonists
In love with their own divinity (like me,
Apotheosis round the corner
Sometimes on good days).

Quotations, pages of them, from the wrong men
Naming the Gods with new jubilance,
Going tandem on the paradox.
'Let us enter', says Pico, 'into the light of ignorance';
'Blindness', says another, 'is the inspiration of the eye!'

And madness more than sanity. Somewhere
The Blessed sit drunken to an eternal feast.
Who but Venus and Minerva crowns the Faun
Blessed with annihilation pouring forth
His dithyrambs, enigmas of Blind Love?
And why does all this rubbish chime with me

Who see soberly the orgy die?
Where was I going on a gust like that? And so
Much trivia round, the daily stuff,
Appointments, people forgotten, a neat row
Of telephone numbers empty now
As any bombed-out terrace in the town:

Lines of verse too left littering
After poems that never got underway.
A pen drawing, very odd, the Storm God Zu
Trussed in his fowl form to a carrying pole;
(From him the wren-walk on St Stephen's Day)

Copied, I suppose, to prove a point.
(Akkadian seal, Babylonian cylinder?) How
Much at home I am in this mad world
Suddenly and again! And here somewhere
You the girl enter

Anonymously, in two wooden stanzas, into which
You have entirely disappeared. Words, words,
That's all you are, girl who never
Was a lover. And I likened you,
Body I could see through, to a catapult

Pulled tight and launching;
(Pinching shamelessly another poet's image)
But also to a hill pipe, as if your flesh was lost
To the air. Amor, amor,
Where has love gone from the cry of old men

That I have to imagine you afresh, as if
I sat there in the Custom House window over
The salt harbour, a young man?
And is it really better
To rage than remain aloof and

Ignore you, never again to
Relearn the resonances? Amor modus
Perpetuus et copula mundi. The
Magnificence, Proclus, Iamblichus, Porphyry,
And the nonsense.

Ambiguous territory for the halt and lame.
Wounds bleed forever. Move on before
A red heart shakes the bone structure. Here is
Excerpt and excerpt. 'Eros jouant avec
Un Masque de Sileni'. Now where did I get that?

And Venus as a Mater dolorosa!
'Not milk', she says, 'do you suck, O savage child,
But the tears of things'. And, my God, Theocritus –
Love and Death exchanging arrows, young
Men die and old men fall in love.

No decorum in the universe.
Sit in the draught, old Body, dream away
And between stumbles make your bit of verse:
No decorum in the universe,
That's what I say

Closing the diary of yesterday's man.
The bay blues the eye; below
Wages a quayside memory, the Frau
Of the Dutch Captain's hanging out her wash,
So young, so young, transfiguring me.

Name Plate

for Helen

My name plate is
Largely outsize, and since it was presented to me
The night I was born by
An unknown woman, something of a mystery

Who saw her at my cradle side
I don't remember. There were no strangers in town,
No circus or penny gaff,
No one, indeed, unaccounted for, yet here she was

Leaning over me with a glitter
Out of her January fur, and this thing in her hand;
Good fairy, said my mother
Later, and promptly decided I'd make a Doctor,

Or a Vet or a Dentist, even a Solicitor
My titles on lasting brass;
And I never gave it a thought, just soldiering on
Nameless, almost anonymous; now and then

Plagued by the vision of a woman leaning over me
Holding out this bit of raw silver
That disappeared in the moonlight, leaving
A most extraordinary nudity.

Argo Left

Up river, silting over, dies
The crestfallen craft, the global outrigger
Shelved and forgotten,
Concerned no more with large affairs
In this world or another;

And no one knows exactly where.
The shag can perch upon a wooden head
Rotting slowly
That once upon a time was rampant god
And no accomplice to mere matter.

This sailor had its living furniture,
Heroes in trim,
Before the flag died on the flagstaff and
The sea forgot to swim
And the rainbow went back into the water.

Friends, what happened? Is the halo of the martyr
No headgear for a man?
Will nobody carry on, be blind
And deaf to all save a mad prompting when
The reason for the trumpets lies behind?

Dardanelles 1916

Last night in stomped
Our Connaught Ranger, Private Patrick Carty
On his way:
                    Fully accoutred now, a ramp
Of belts and bandoliers, a bayonet
Wags at his side with no wound yet, the heavy
Haversack sits high:

                    Filling the back kitchen, squinting
Down from the roofbeams, shyly
Shaking hands all round the family, smiling;
Me he picks up and by God kisses me.

                    Up there under
The brown-white plaster an unknown soldier's face
Is weeping.

                    Do I remember more? The urchin daughters
Bold for once and peeping
Washed and ribboned through the door to wave
Him off on the Mail, the 4.15, and away
Where muted now in a long sand he lies, if not
Entirely melted into
The steadfast bony glare of Asia Minor.

One Easter Morning

The first Ephebe thunderstruck between
The maidenhead and the mother sweats with fear:
Narcissus drops eternal anchor here,
The swathed genital the dangerous theme;

Already he carries the thousand years of me,
My broken nakedness, my old-age cry;
And I the lonely terror of the boy,
Unable for Mother Ogre and the mystery.

In between are the lover's years. Forgive
The time that never found the clockfaced moon
Chime with the moment that brings us two alive,

That brings to love the fabulous young head
And love's own body to an ageing man,
To you the gold shower and the vast untrammelled bed.

Encounter at Penshurst

To come by her thus, by accident,
In the Sidney bailiwick, in apple Kent,
And be taken

In her happening, in the old man-pull;
Witch, in her meridian, sitting under
The Greenwich tree,

Gold, russet, she was luminous they say;
And here but a very small bronze
Death mask, beaked as a prow

Where shamelessly aquiver I hang
Over a queen, baited by the
Tiny Eidolon,

Sinking towards the mouth with all
Those earls and groomsmen, jostling for room –
At a lover's height there is no death

But one face in the ecliptic. (Some
Necrophilia certainly.) I do
Commune in some love act

With her sailing island perhaps, its Drakes and drums
Forgetting the railing shrew
For the narrow stomacher, the woman's writ in the red hair,

Even the old royal raddled idol wishing England up
Out on the galleoned seas into
The new geography.

Homeric Hymns

The Stealing of Apollo's Cattle

The maid Maia shook her head, here is
No cattle reiver, my lord Apollo, come
And see;

    And there was only
An empty cavern. Wait,
There was in the very plush centre
Tiny as a beam
Of sunlight in a pinhole, a small
Gold cradle that rocked itself.

My son, said the maid, a true
Lovechild to Zeus;
        And indeed there glowed
In the blues and saffrons of the quilts one
Small triumphant head.
        But three days old, said the maid.
And it seemed to the god
The air was filled with the lowing
Of cattle. Maiden, he said, my herds
Are nearby. Where?
        The thief was here,
Here he stood, so recently I can hear
Heifers chew the cud and drop dung –
        Maiden, said Apollo.

My Lord, said the bare truth in her, only Zeus
Comes here.

My cattle were or are in this cavern.

Lord, is Zeus a reiver?

                    The god
was staring at the infant in the cot.
Three days, he said, three days old and
Already a monster.
                    Wake up, my newest brother,
And talk to me.
                    Take your choice. Speak or
I throw you downstairs to Tartarus.
                                        I see
I do not discommode you, little thief.
                    He shook the cradle noting
How the child rode it, all the rough and tumble.

So, child, you too are a power. In that case,
Let us speak as equals.

A great voice filled the cavern.
                    My brother is
Too kind. How may we speak as man to man with this
Wet dribble down my chin?

Thunder in Heaven, said Apollo, you could be Heracles.

That thumper, said the babe. No, thank you. Could he
Hide from your all-seeing eye the two cowskins
I pegged outside to dry?

                    My cows, the god whispered, the
Sacred ones.

                    Who sacrificed when I was born? said the babe.
With Zeus, terrified of his old termagant, hiding
Us here in the wilderness.

                    My child, my child, said Maia.

What other sacrifice would have relevance to
A major birth like mine?
                    What other
Shake the heavens, give the place a new
Tilt?

Apollo hung over him in two wide wings.
You laugh, Babe, do you laugh at me?

No, said the little lad, should a child
Three days old, take on the big loud-spoken
Almighties? I haven't finished my
Disquisition with reference to your kine.

          The child sat up. He
Was quite luminous, already stretched
Far beyond the body.
                    I thought, said he,
That heaven too should rejoice when I was born.
So I sacrificed your heifers to the Gods,
To the Twelve.

Apollo said, I see you want me to state
That we Olympians number only
Eleven.
              So the twelfth smoke
Arises for a three-day-old, a babe?

Ho, said the child, you shall have your cattle back
At once.

My cattle, Apollo answered, I have already.
Look into your mind, you will not find them there.

The child pondered. That's a trick, a right one
You'll have to teach me.

Some say, said Apollo,
With birch and ferrule. Well, I'm pleased
In one way to have met you, Number Twelve.
Goodbye.

You'll be back, said the babe.

The maiden Maia walked with the god, her face
Was full of wonder.
                    What can I say, my Lord Apollo?

Behind, in the cave, the earth had begun
To dance, Apollo turned:
            A child making the music,
                                    from
A shell, a simple shell
            (And that was the first string plucked)

I thought you'd be back, said the little one.
All desires pull.
                  And you want my shell. Here.

The music died, Apollo took the shell
Divining it,
            But could not find his way into a tune.

You'll have to teach me, said he.
Some say, said the babe,
With birch and ferrule. And one must be a god of course.
Trees do not dance for common people.

O little cattle-robber, would you roast
Apollo in the sun?

            He laughed, the laughter going forth
In thunders that rapped the stone heads of hills
And rained in the valleys.

            Teach me, little brother, birch
Your sorry elder, but there's an art I must have.

You have it, said the Babe. Now
Quid pro quo, your royal herds for me.

Hey, said Apollo.

            The music stopped.
                  So, said Apollo, you can stop me
A simply as that.

While the herds are yours, the gift and the shell
Are mine.

Ah, sighed the great god. I'll take the shell.
But tell me, wonder-babe, what will you do
With cattle, they're no toys, they're not exactly
Cradle playthings, what will you do with them?

Eat them, said the little lad. And grow up
To be like Daddy.
           This time however I reserve
The twelve best portions for myself, for Hermes,
He said modestly, the youngest and perhaps the fairest
Of the Gods.

Rape of Persephone

And Zeus allowed it,
The Thunderer.
That the lord of Hell should know the touch of woman
In the groping shades:

Therefore this
Narcissus flower was born for her,
In the innocent grass
A most delicate snare;

It was alive, living;
A fountain of blossom;
And it grew just beyond her hand;
Tempting.

A servant could have plucked it:
She could have called,
But the buds seemed to jet
And be lost, only
To come again and be always there
In the presence:

It was the Presence caught her;
Hypnosis of
The whole person;
Lost, that was it, she was lost in
Her own flowering.

Then the mandate of the male
Reached her, earth
Was cloven at her feet, declivity
After declivity;

And everything, inside and out, was happening;
There was this man-head in her
Woman-body,

And vice-versa, she
Was the savage male she peacefully assuaged
In love's small handiwork.

Now as one they go
Gold chariot
Lighting something far beyond themselves.

To Pan

There's a lynx skin
On the fellow's back. He sleeps raw
Has many terms of reference he denies,
Being in two
Places at once;

And not quite Olympian,
Indeed a very
Haphazard itinerant, shy of the main roads
You could pass him by where
He gossips in a wayside smoke.

But mark his face in
Your apple tree, that'll be dawn or dusk.
Only remember he has a dozen more
And can sit down with any simple girl
And turn her into a whore.

And how he dances full-bobbined on a well
With the Muses in the wild
Array he spreads around, and
The lovely girls are scattered, garments strewn
About him on the ground.

The entire lilting world will follow him.
Don't grudge your wife,
And let the budding girl foot the fallow;
Hoof and horns are good
In field and wood.

If the childless hear
The distant fluting clear and thin,
Wombs open. Here's the seed
Drops out of heaven on the ray of morning,
And the end of need.

Pan call him, Hermes' boy,
Capricorn has built him from the earliest
Model, from bits and pieces of the scrap-heaped gods,
A leftover, but the face
Was born of itself, is full of grace.

After Pindar

The Hyperboreans

Among them too are the Muses
For everywhere
To flute and string the young girls
Are dancing,
In their hair the gold leaves of the bay:

The dance whirls them away:
Age or disease, no toil,
Battle or ill-day's luck
Can touch them, they
Are holy, they
Will outlast time, exempted
From the anger of the Goddess
And all decay.

Here the hero came
With the head
That shocked a royal house, turning
King and all into stone:
It was long ago, if
Time means anything;
Long, long ago.

The Infant Heracles

Two serpents she sent,
Hera, Mother of the Gods,
And the child barely out of the womb

Lying haphazard like his twin brother
(Which was the immortal one?)
At his mother's bedside:

Doors opened to the great worms;
(There is no sanctuary from the gods)
Their shuffling rings in the midnight house
Scarcely a sibilance:

And nobody cried out in nightmare
When their fanged heads
Flickered at the cradle top;
No one gave the alarm;
The household slept;

But one child, a never-sleeper, crowed
And took from the air in growing and terrible hands
The sinister strikers;
By the napes he shook them
Till the wincing coils went slack,

And dropped them, like old rope, his twin
Bawling beside him, waking up
A commotion, which

Mounted Olympus, waking thrones,
And all the gods stared down while one looked up,
A new one

No longer indistinguishable, though
He shared the soothing dug with mortal flesh
And fell asleep.

After Theocritus

With the Gift of a Distaff

Good distaff, sprung first
From a whorl of Athena's thumb, Theocritus
Your poet is for Miletus, dingle of the Goddess, the
Love-woman of Kypris, and
Begs your company:

Have no fear of the uncertain sea;
Though Zeus distribute the uneven world
To every wind, beyond
The loom of the last island is our city and
Journey's end in
A friend's heart:

My comrade Nikias waits there for me;
And for you, Theugenis, his young wife who hails
From Syracuse, our own birthplace, the very
Navel of Sicily;
A simple girl full of grace.

O pleasing little ivory give yourself
To this lady, if only for a year,
And shepherds will double their flocks if only to keep pace with you,
And hill farmers
Look to the ram, for with you two as partners

Cloaks will dance off the buzzing loom
And precious undergarments hang
On the woman's line:
Distaff, I offer you no slattern's dwelling:
Here things live by the book

And Nikias holds forth, a master of medicine
Famous for his cures;
This is a notable house and I offer it

That my countrywoman, Theugenis, be renowned
For a distaff of such quality
That she must remember when she uses it
The poet, the giver,
Her visitor once, the singer of songs;

And Ionian housekeepers who see you spin
So large round such a tiny heart shall say,
'This, indeed, is a true gift
That multiplies itself in such
Huge increases day after day'.

After Callimachus

Erysichton

There was this youth who was I
And no way to dare
The Gods and bring them to the eye,
And make them aware.

So into her grave, axe high, I drove
The lovely body I was, the royal make,
And plucked her tree by tree;
The poplar first:

Be naked, I said, like me;
Match me in thigh, in eye, in high
Profile, and let one lose the other
In every form until we find the one;
What's love but the destruction of the world,
The unity of all in nothing?

She was there;
No lover, no mother, a woman,
That's all she was,

Composing my parts, a simple woman
Touching on all my points, enhancing
The little things I had forgotten;

My touch the more delicate, my eyes
A drift of the everyday most various world;
Stay this, I said. Let be.

But all of her was motion, she
Was passing, on the move and away, not
To be held,
The colours of seasons, the commons of the day,
Seen, wondered on, taken in
Most blindly indoors,
Where a woman should be
And a hearth.

That was the newest hunger,
To absorb her.

A life's work,
The appetite more and more. I ate
Up cities, my heart
Grabbed at states and realms, sprawled on
Continents,

While I lost sight and flesh and motion
And sit now
Bony hand out on the roadside.
Begging.

And nobody sees her;
All those passers-by with their small coins
And birds' eggs
Going up to the city

Walk right through the enormous body
That straddles the highway
That is Demeter my lady, my
Eternal hunger.

After Horace

Solvitur Acris Hiems

The first soft zephyr loosens the snowman's grip;
Ships roll down to the sea;
Cows leave the straw, the ploughman his ingle-nook;
The new pastures gaze through melting frost;

And Venus arrives in the sailing moon, with a wave
Of dancers, nymphs and Graces linked
To a naked beat, earth thrumming, while lame Vulcan spells
The blazing Cyclops at the furnaces.

And it's time to mingle in the happening, sport a twig
Of myrtle or a spring flower,
And remember Faunus with a lamb or a young kid,
Whichever he prefer:

For Death, dear Sestius, is always that much closer;
In hovel or tower a door
Will open of itself, there's no escaping, here
He stands with his phantoms waiting:

And no lucky throw will make you lord of a feast
Ever again; the dice are dead, the boy
Lycidas left to delight your enemy's eye
And all those girls at his feet.

After the Archpoet

(Twelfth Century)

Confessio

Great anger shakes me.
I must allow it tongue;
Hear me then, you men
Not yet hanged damned or wrung.
I am made of light matter,
Light as a leaf, with the wings
Of a leaf and blown as one;
No longer my own master.

A wise man rides a thought,
Reins, unreins the steady horse;
But when I ride the saddle's
Just one more wing on my arse;
Any stir releases
The kites in me, O God
The air discourses no more
Than I in windy weather.

Thoughts mutiny, I stamp my poop,
Find no answer in the crew;
The sails take over up there
Like bird or cloud, blow through the blue;
No bonds, keys, gods
Can lock away my mind;
My thoughts deprave me, drive me
To seek my sinful kind.

The heavy weight of man
Has no room on my shoulders;
I seek the honeycomb, and must
Advance in roses;
Venus naked as a cloud
Or drenched in the coloured sea-wash moves
Me like a white shell shoreward,
Yet looms in the brightness leeward.

Before me, she. In the broad way
A glimpse where my youth goes;
She uses so many bodies
That turn to empty phrases;
Clichés! The flesh can't stand up
To all her meanings, her sudden poses;
She's sold me many a pup.
How do I still stand up?

And now again, smitten again; in love
With a young thing! Your pardon, Lord,
But here's the flower must heap my grave.
This girl's your earliest word,
You spoke it in the garden to a tree;
Here she is and I go down
Before your creation on one knee.
Here she is and I go down.

And ask nothing. O difficult to deny
This old boy raging in my skin.
A virgin! And I on one knee!
O Goddess, kick me on the shin,
Let Goatfoot take me over, Pan
Make tinwhistles of my thighbones;
Sing my shame among the fairies, but
My two knees are sinking down.

For this is Pavia. And you, friend,
You'll come, expecting to go chaste
Home, unburned, untarnished? What a hope,
Where every day's a waste
If Venus doesn't blossom in
A door or fill a street with
The marvellous body that shook the gate
Of Heaven – if we can believe the myth.

But try it, bring Hippolytus,
Chaste Hippolytus, to Pavia;
Give him the reins – and see him eat the bridle;
Look for him *sequente die*,
In the first light, or the second light. No
Hippolytus, bird flown.
For of all the towers in Pavia there's none
Was raised to chastity, not one.

You raise, too, the matter of my gambling.
Right, I admit. The dawn and I
Have shared a naked bench together
With the first snail horning at the sky
Often, Boy, and my only coat in pawn;
And yet with the frost at full bite have found
Such profundity, forgotten it
In the heat of verse, the beaten anvil's sound.

My drinking too? Don't leave that out.
Impeach me – liquidly.
I'm given to it, yield without fight.
My measures don't lack quantity.
What if a second head comes over mine,
The drunken mask of Faunus, he's a friend;
When angels sing my requiem,
He'll be there, Boy, puking to the end.

Meum est propositum – I mean
In the vernacular, let me die drunk
Struck by Jove's thunderstone the bottle,
After some words with that same lordly skunk.
If you're given to angels, here you'll see them
Heartbroken, their feathers round me,
Singing, God is good to this
Tavern fellow, *huic polatori.*

A lamp shines in the cup.
It animates the ghost
That gives, on second thoughts, a fellow wings
To meet (on second thoughts) the holy host.
Sweet is the glass I pour
In my sacred corner with a whore,
A halo on it, wings, no mitre.
(The bishop's stuff but feeds a goitre.)

I know that poets full of grace
Should leave the tavern to the fool;
I know that poets full of grace
Should leave the forum to the fool;
I know that poets full of grace
Should pare the quill, prepare the ink,
Write epics with a pious face;
And never never die of drink.

Dear Friend, it's not that way at all.
Good verse never wore
Its halo with a saintly tilt.
When did Apollo love a bore?
Is a hungry belly free to think?
Where does a rhyme start? On whose feet
Does Bacchus stagger out to drink?
Don't the heavens sup when a poet stands treat?

So fast you for me, since I
Must spread my rhymes from a full bag.
If guts are hollow wind accrues,
Fast you for me;
With your great gift for nothing hunger goes,
Therefore fast, boy;
And let me fatten against the rutting time
When poems mill round me like wild does.

And that's my case, my head
Plain on the platter. All can see now
The errors of my soulcase.
I do accuse myself.
But add to this; I'm judge and jury, Lord,
And in all dignity look down my throne
On the drunken whoremongering sinner, Me,
And passing sentence say, Live on, Live on!

After Gérard de Nerval

Vers Dorés

One for Helen

Man the Thinker! You think yourself the sole
Thinker in a world where all things think to be?
The powers you are have given you liberty,
But you leave Nature out that makes the whole:

Regard the beast and how a spirit moves him;
Each flower hatched by the humble earth's a soul;
In metals repose Love's mystery and fall:
All's sensible, cries Pythagoras. We share a dream.

The eye looks out on you from a blind wall;
In matter the Holy Word is working still –
Careful! it's delicate and must serve no ill.

Often the god inhabits the dark inside,
Under night's lids the great light-bearing ball,
Under the skins of stones the living tide.

After Baudelaire

The Cat

My time was then, before Earth tamed volcanoes
To fold their petals quietly as a rose,
When from her loves Nature had who knows
What strange children in mighty ebbs and flows.

I could have been a cat, voluptuously
Curious on the knees of a huge young queen
While she flowered in large sweet tremors under me,
Wooed but wondering, lost, and longingly obscene.

To trouble her look with a male and secret stare,
Green as glass, and then, O love, to wander
The great valleys of her loosening knees

Or sometimes in summer evenings when she rests
Stretched out like a countryside, to take my ease
Like a sleepy mountain village on her breasts.

Parfum Exotique

Your body this humid afternoon is another
Climate, your breast a tropic I take over,
Geography a sultry odour, aromas of you where
I lie headlong on a new-found equator;

An island listing to the Trades drops fruit
Down the tilted South; big mincing bucks
Laze on the skyline and your blood-sisters flit
By, outstaring me with insolent good looks;

Here are the regions native to your flesh,
A drugged seahaven, ships at the wall
With cockbilled yards, broken from seas too tall;

And the green tamarinds, the odour of – and the mess –
Mix in the salt world drifting off your skin
With the sailaway chanties of the deepwater men.

A Bird for Nancy

(L'Albatros)

Often for devilment old salts might snare
An albatross, the big white ocean bird
Following after, supreme voyager,
Dangling his indolent carriage over the surge.

Scarcely is the great winged creature down
Than the grace goes; a flapping huddled thing
On wooden pinions oaring itself along,
The flight, the royal repose, the tilt all gone.

This feathered traveller how maladroit afoot,
Fellow of the air, so lately beautiful;
One thrusts a smoking claypipe down his throat;
And one apes the flight of the poor earthbound fool.

And that's the image, Poet; a prince in the air
You laugh down the gale at the archer and his bow;
But on earth a butt for every hoot and stare,
Wings useless, and no real place to go.

Two Mallarmé Things for Sue

1

The flesh is sad. I have read all the books.
It's a jacked-up world. Even the birds sling their hooks.
And I could do with a trip to unknown skies;

There's nothing. Even the gardens of your eyes,
No lie, hold my glance no more. The damp's
In everything, even the lamp's
Empty room on the white page. (The poem's
Dead against me, help me God.) Home's
No longer where the doll is dishing out
The baby's bowl of stout.
                              I'll leave, by Christ
The next boat's mine. I'll see I keep the tryst.

Bored to the tits, sick of the same old guff,
I'd love a whole dockland to wave me off.
The winds are welcome to my perch;
I know the earth by my legs' sea-lurch;
It's shipwrecked, Mates, and heaved along
By nothing more than a sailor's song.

Primitive spring lays winter in sad waste,
My most civil winter, season of lucid things;
And in my distressed man the new tide brings
The impotence of a world gone double-faced.

The white corpuscles roar round my head;
I've haloes of iron on my unlaurelled brow;
I'm the sad joker with the unbent bow
In the broad champaigns where the dews can raise the dead.

The huge mad dancing dews, and me with a dream
Following after, falling unnerved to the trees,
Given to the earth and the odours, going along with the stream.

I bite holes where lilacs must sink roots,
And know how I beam when my hedges blow to the breeze
And birds in a thousand blossoms clamour on the shoots.

After Rimbaud

Ma Bohême

So I tramped the roads, my hands through my torn pockets
My old coat just a ghost about to vanish;
I was your tramp, Muse, but rich, with worlds to lavish,
La, la, the marvels we dream of, we mad poets!

I rhymed with my buttocks falling out like moons
Through holes in my trousers, uncaring, my head in the air;
I took a room each night in the Great Bear;
Stars over my distant hair had the soft swish of gowns.

And I listened, excited with dew as with strong wine,
At my ease in a ditch, a mood, a creature of starshine
In the good September twilights, a man apart,

And rhyming, rhyming, while all the darks took root,
I tucked one leg like a lyre about my heart
And strummed the elastic of my broken boot.

O Saisons, O Châteaux

O Seasons, O Châteaux,
What angel is there will not fall low?

O Seasons, O Châteaux,

I have made a magic study
Of the good thing that eludes nobody;

Sing it every time you hear
The gallic cock its chanticleer;

Me, I have no will at all,
It's taken me over body and soul,

A spell usurping whatever I be
Blows all abroad, dispersing me,

So that to understand a word
You flee and follow like a bird.

Seasons O, and O Châteaux.

After the Medieval Irish

Columcille the Scribe

My hand is weary with writing;
The light quill twitters in my fingers;
Yet here, still, my slender-mouthed pen
Pours a draught for me of dark-blue ink.

My brown hand – O blessed it is indeed
With the stream of God's wisdom pouring from it! –
Squirting the brightness of many inks,
Moves happily till leaf after leaf is lit.

Ah, my little pen, it moves on
Across the plain of books in holy words,
And without ceasing makes, though I am tired,
Cyphers that suddenly take wings like birds.

Biographical Note

1905 Padraic Fallon is born in Athenry, Co. Galway, 3 January, the son of John Fallon, a prosperous cattle and sheep 'jobber', and his wife Ellen, née Dillon. He is the second child of the marriage, the eldest being his sister Bridget ('Billy'). There are seven siblings in all, of whom four survive into adulthood. The family also owns a butcher's shop in the town and his mother runs a small hotel.

1917–23 Goes as a boarder to Mount St Joseph's, Roscrea in Co. Tipperary (run by Cistercians). Is so unhappy there that his family moves him to the diocesan college at Ballinasloe, much nearer home (see the poem 'Stop on the Road to Ballylee'). Meanwhile the Irish War of Independence is fought, followed by the Civil War of 1922–3. His own family is staunchly Home Rule, but he himself is excited by the nationalist and republican ferment. Proves to be an outstanding athlete, adept at sprinting, hurling and handball, as well as a competent horseman.

1923 Passes the entrance exam for the Irish civil service and begins work with the Customs and Excise, based in Gandon's eighteenth-century Custom House on the Dublin quays. Meets Æ (George William Russell), a leading figure of the Literary Revival, who encourages him and gets his first poems published. Æ also influences him in the direction of oriental philosophy and mysticism. Continues his athletic activities, winning various prizes and medals. Under the influence of Frank Duff, a prominent Catholic layman, engages in social work in the Dublin slums on behalf of the Society of St Vincent de Paul. Meanwhile, his father, suffering from deafness and depression, lapses into bankruptcy and the family moves to Dublin.

These years are a period of avid reading, including the discovery of Yeats's poetry. Meets Yeats himself on at least two occasions, through Æ, but finds him rather cold and aloof. As well as verse, writes short stories, and probably tries his hand at playwriting.

1930 Marries Dorothea ('Don') Maher, daughter of a Dublin builder, and takes up a posting in Cootehill, Co. Cavan, close to the border with Northern Ireland. Son Garret (died 1996) is born in 1931, and a second son, Brian, is born in 1933. During this period he is visited by the poet Patrick Kavanagh, who cycles over from neighbouring Co. Monaghan, and in return visits Kavanagh on his mother's farm.

1936 Resumes official work in Dublin while living in Sutton, just north of the capital. Writes regularly for the *Dublin Magazine* and becomes a close friend of its editor, Seumas O'Sullivan, and his wife, the gifted painter Estella Solomons. Also friendly with the poets Patrick MacDonogh, Austin Clarke and F.R Higgins. Reputation begins to grow.

1939 Birth of son Conor. Moves to Wexford, on the south-east coast, living at first on the edge of the town but the following year (1940) moves to another house in a more rural setting. Deeply affected by the outbreak of the Second World War, during which his official duties bring him into contact with the bodies of drowned sailors and even of German airmen. With petrol rationing in force, he occasionally cycles to and from Dublin, ninety miles distant. A fourth son, Niall (died 1996), is born in 1941. Starts to study French, without a teacher.

1944 Moves to a house in Wexford town where his fifth son, Ivan, is born. Continues to read French, particularly Baudelaire and Rimbaud, both of whom he translates. Sixth son, Padraic, born in 1946. Studies the poetry of Rilke in English translation. Does a good deal of sailing in a small open boat.

1948 Moves to an eighteenth-century house outside the town, called Prospect, which will be his home for fifteen years. The house has twenty acres attached, which he farms with the help of his sons. Writes the radio play *Diarmuid and Grainne*, which is eventually broadcast by Radio Eireann in 1950 and is an instant success. (Later it is broadcast by the BBC Third Programme.) This is followed by others: *The Vision of Mac Conglinne*, *The Poplar*, *The Wooing of Etain*, etc.

1954 Play *The Seventh Step* produced in Cork and Dublin. Though the work is highly praised by some critics, Fallon is dissatisfied and eventually withdraws it. Nevertheless, continues to have ambitions to write for the stage.

1963 Puts Prospect on the market and moves to Dublin, living in the suburb of Dartry. Begins to write the meditative, distanced poetry of his 'third period'. Feels somewhat apart from the younger generation of Irish poets, who are mainly influenced by Auden and various American models.

1967 Takes early retirement from the Civil Service. Moves to Cornwall, where his son Conor is already living, as is his old friend the painter Tony O'Malley. Lives in a rural area near Penzance. Failing health – he undergoes two serious operations, the second of which costs him one of his lungs – begins to take its toll. Nevertheless, continues to write verse.

1971 Play *Sweet Love Till Morn* staged at the Abbey Theatre in Dublin, but has only a brief run.

1972 Moves back to Ireland and settles in Kinsale, Co. Cork. Works on a book of poems and translations for Carcanet Press, which he does not live to see in print.

1974   In summer the Dolmen Press in Dublin – shortly to go bankrupt – finally brings out the long-deferred *Collected Poems*, after a delay of several years. While visiting his son Ivan in Kent, he contracts pneumonia – a death sentence for a man with one lung. Dies in hospital at Aylsford shortly before midnight on 8 October. His body is taken back to Kinsale and buried in a graveyard facing the Atlantic. On his wife's death in 1985, she is buried beside him.

Notes on the Poems

Page 2 'Yeats's Tower at Ballylee'. On a motor tour of the West of Ireland, Fallon visited the tower during the wet summer of 1950. It was then in a forlorn and dilapidated condition – the poet and his wife George had more or less shut it up twenty years before – but it has since been fully restored and is now a place of pilgrimage. The war imagery refers to the fighting in Korea, which many people saw then as a major step towards a third world war.

Page 8 'Poem for my Mother'. Killimore-Daly, in the rather flat and monotonous countryside of East Galway, is pronounced Kill-eye-mer. The reference to Aughrim is to the battle fought there in 1691, when the Jacobite cause in Ireland suffered a terminal defeat. According to a family tradition, a number of brothers who were ancestors of the poet's mother (born Ellen Dillon) died in this battle.

Page 15 'Vowels'. See Rimbaud's poem 'Voyelles'. During the 1940s and 1950s, Fallon was an avid reader of this poet.

Page 16 'Dialogue between Raftery and Death'. The blind Gaelic tramp-poet Anthony Raftery, who wrote in the first third of the nineteenth century, was very much part of local folklore in the area of Co. Galway where Fallon grew up. Raftery lost his sight at the age of nine, but the apparition of Death one night was said to have temporarily restored it. Fallon made him the central character in his radio play *The Bell for Mister Loss*, and also translated his popular love poem 'Mary Hynes' as well as 'Raftery's Dialogue with the Whiskey'.

Page 23 'Maud Gonne'. Fallon did in fact enjoy at least one lengthy tête-à-tête with the (English-born) nationalist heroine, the widow of John MacBride and muse of Yeats. The poem first appeared in the *Bell* magazine of February 1952, little more than a year before her death.

Page 27 'A Flask of Brandy'. A childhood memory of Athenry. All his life the poet was a lover of circuses.

Page 28 'The Head'. Written during the early 1950s, this poem was rediscovered in a drawer more than a decade later. The oracular imagery obviously relates both to the Orpheus myth and the singing head of Bran – mythic themes which form the central poetic plank in Fallon's radio play *The Vision of MacConglinne*.

Page 34 'Tradesman's Entrance'. These lyrics originally formed part of the radio play *A Man in the Window*. Fallon first arranged them in their present sequence for the Dolmen Press *Collected Poems* of 1974.

Pages 36–7 'Meeting' and 'Field Observation'. Both based on real life countrymen whom the poet met almost daily while walking or driving between his home a few miles outside Wexford town, and the Customs and Excise office on the town quays.

Page 38 'Johnstown Castle'. The castle is a neo-Gothic building standing in spacious grounds with an ornamental lake, a few miles from Wexford town. The 'old lady' was its last private occupant, Lady Fitzgerald; after her death in 1946 it became a state agricultural college.

Page 42 'March Twentysix'. Written after the funeral in 1958, at Mount Jerome cemetery in Dublin, of the poet and man of letters Seumas O'Sullivan (James Sullivan Starkey), for many years editor of the *Dublin Magazine* in which Fallon published regularly from the 1930s onwards.

Page 43 'River Lane'. Based on a real-life woman and local 'character' in Callan, Co. Kilkenny. Fallon learned about her from anecdotes told to him by his close friend, the painter Tony O'Malley (1913–2003), who was born there.

Page 49 'Weir Bridge'. The stone bridge over the River Corrib in Galway city, familiar to the poet since childhood. See also Louis MacNeice's poem 'Closing Album' (1939). George Moore in the 'Salve' volume of his 'Hail and Farewell' trilogy describes how he, Yeats and Edward Martyn had watched the same sight of the migrating salmon a generation earlier.

Page 50 'Gowran Park, Autumn Meeting'. A well-known racecourse in Co. Kilkenny, pronounced 'Goran'. Like various other Irish writers such as Liam O'Flaherty, Francis Stuart and Anthony Cronin, Fallon was a keen follower of the Turf, especially in his later years.

Page 51 'The Young Fenians'. Originally written for a TV documentary commemorating the (rather abortive) Fenian uprising of the 1860s. Daniel O'Connell was, of course, dead by then but probably his name is used in a generic sense to represent the tradition of non-violent nationalism which the Fenians rejected – just as, half a century later, the 1916 Easter Rebellion effectively killed off the parliamentary Home Rule tradition.

Page 51 'Capricornian'. Fallon was himself born under the sign of Capricorn (21 December–19 January). 'That old poet' is Horace, and the phrase 'found spring wells holy' refers simultaneously to Horace's Bandusian spring and to the 'holy wells' found throughout Ireland. To an island community, of course, a spring of 'sweet water' could be a matter of life and death.

Page 53 'A Visit West'. Fallon paid a number of visits to Athenry, his birthplace, and adjacent areas during the 1960s. 'Old Ben' was his unmarried paternal uncle, a difficult man who by then was aged, crabbed and bedridden. The Homeric image of the wooden horse is presumably a symbol of the socio-political revolution which had brought the former 'wild Irish' within the confines of a Norman-Irish town, previously dominated by Protestant gentry and merchants.

Page 55 'Boyne Valley'. The River Boyne, which mainly flows through Co. Meath north of Dublin, is famous in Irish history and legend and its reaches are rich in tumuli and prehistoric remains. Here Fallon meditates on the nature of myth and, in particular, on the ancient ritual of sacrificing a kingly victim at Midsummer Eve (see Frazer's *The Golden Bough* and Robert Graves's *The White Goddess*, both of which were in his library). 'Scantlings' were lopped poles or slender treetrunks used by builders before the advent of metal scaffolding, and 'the barnacle' is the barnacle goose. Cernunnos was an ancient Celtic (or Gaulish) underworld deity.

Page 58 'Kiltartan Legend'. Plainly, Lady Gregory, and not the wife of Odysseus, is the real subject of this poem.

Page 59 'Yeats at Athenry Perhaps'. That Fallon as a boy may have glimpsed Yeats in this way, without knowing who or what he was, is perfectly feasible. The railway station at Athenry was, and still is, the first stop along the line for people travelling east from Galway city, about ten miles distant, across the Midlands to Dublin. Yeats, whether living in his Ballylee tower or staying with Lady Gregory at Coole Park near Gort, presumably would have driven to Gort station, immediately to the south, and from there proceeded to Athenry to make the connection with the Dublin-bound train.

Page 62 'Stop on the Road to Ballylee'. Written at the time of Yeats's centenary in 1965, when Fallon – then living in Dublin – visited the west of Ireland with his wife. The setting is the town of Ballinasloe where Fallon had gone to boarding school decades before; after the school had moved to another location nearby, the original building became a lunatic asylum. The inmates apparently are viewed as souls astray between two worlds, like the unburied dead of classical times, and the various quotations from Horace include an indirect one from Odes Book I, XXVII, in which the ghost of a drowned sailor pleads for the ritual sprinkling of a few handfuls of sea-sand on his corpse. Mingled with this, in a kind of intricate counterpoint, are memories of Fallon's schooldays and of his first readings of Horace, who became his favourite poet in the last decade and a half of his life.

Page 64 'On the Tower Stairs'. Once again, the subject is Lady Gregory. Yeats's poet-friend Arthur Symonds used to refer to her in private as the *strega* (witch); for a semi-humorous description of Yeats's attempts at magic-making at Coole see Moore's 'Hail and Farewell'. To Fallon, Lady Gregory was essentially a local personage

146

since she and her family, the Persses of Roxborough, were well known in and around Athenry. 'Biblical household' refers to their proselytising Protestantism. 'Husband-father': Augusta Persse was thirty-five years younger than her husband, Sir Robert Gregory of Coole Park, Gort, who had been governor of both Egypt and Ceylon. His grandfather had been Under-Secretary for Ireland and Lady Gregory edited a selection of his correspondence under the title *Mr Gregory's Letter-Box, 1813–1830*. She was not in fact her husband's biographer but edited his memoirs, which appeared posthumously. 'That bronze' presumably refers to the portrait head of Lady Gregory executed by Epstein.

Page 66 'The Small Town of John Coan'. The poems began life as incidental lyrics to Fallon's radio play *Two Men with a Face*. The central theme of this work is the strange attraction-repulsion between a small-town businessman and a local halfwit in whom he recognises his own alter ego or *Doppelgänger*. As the lyrics grew detached from their original context, they gradually became in effect a series of inward meditations on small-town life.

Page 73 'Magna Mater'. The words 'a dove plus an assenting virgin' refer to the traditional imagery of the Annunciation and Incarnation, when Mary 'conceived of the Holy Ghost' in the form of a dove. 'The least erotic of the gods' is presumably Christ. The line 'where flowers are born with the name of kings' is a smuggled quotation from the late Roman poet Ausonius.

Page 74 'For Paddy Mac'. The gifted poet Patrick McDonogh (1902–61) was probably the closest of all Fallon's literary friends. After a period in which his sensitive, fastidious talent was neglected, he appears to be coming back into his own and his *Collected Poems* have been reissued by Gallery Press, edited and with a preface by Derek Mahon.

Page 78 'Special for Nancy's Mother'. Written on the occasion of the marriage between the poet's third son Conor – now a prominent Irish sculptor – and the painter Nancy Wynne-Jones. The ceremony took place in 1966 at the bride's parents' house near Dolgellau, in Wales, and Nancy's two dead brothers, Alec and Ronald, are evoked as tutelary spirits of the place in which they had spent most of their childhood. Both were killed on active service during the Second World War. (See *Nancy Wynne-Jones at Eighty*, ed. Brian Fallon, recently published by Gandon Press, Kinsale, Co. Cork.)

Page 80 'Brigid her Eve'. The feast of St Brigid, *La Fheile Bhrighde*, falls on 1 February and is traditionally regarded in parts of rural Ireland as the beginning of spring, or at least the end of winter. Her symbol, the rush cross, is still hung over doors for good luck. In this poem the quasi-historical St Brigid is intermingled with the goddess Brigid or Bride, the Celtic Muse, and the Magna Mater/White Goddess who haunts Fallon's entire output. The dedication is to the poet's son Conor and his wife, Nancy Wynne-Jones.

Page 83 'Lakshmi'. As I remember, my father specifically told me this was suggested by an illustration in the *Larousse Dictionary of Oriental Mythology* (which he pointed out to me), showing a bronze statue of the Hindu goddess. However, my brother Conor also tells me that his wife Nancy once gave my father a small bronze figure of Lakshmi which he kept in his room. Lakshmi or Laksmi was originally an earth deity but later became the goddess of health and good fortune; she is usually depicted holding a lotus, or sometimes seated on an eight-leafed lotus throne. (See *The Illustrated Dictionary of Hindu Iconography* by Margaret Stutley, Routledge, 1985.)

Page 85 'Three Houses'. These dwellings, which are named and evoked in turn, were all farmhouses owned by uncles of the poet by marriage, in which he stayed for periods of his early life, and which were closely associated with scenes and emotions of his childhood and boyhood. All were situated in Co. Galway and have almost vanished in the march of rural progress. 'The old Landleaguer' was Peter Nolan, married to one of Fallon's maternal aunts, who served as the chief model for the figure of Jerome in one of his finest radio plays, *The Poplar*.

Page 91 'Trevaylor'. Fallon moved from Dublin to Cornwall in 1967 and lived there until the early 1970s, when he returned to Ireland for his terminal years. Trevaylor is the name of a large country house at Gulval, near Penzance, acquired by Nancy Wynne-Jones and now an old folks' home. The poet and his wife lived in a house directly opposite.

Page 92 'Painting of My Father'. The painting in question was executed by Fallon's son Conor. The poet's long-lived father, John Fallon, was a successful cattle and sheep 'jobber' in Athenry until premature deafness more or less ended his career in middle age. In his teens the poet frequently accompanied him to the cattle marts in Dublin. The Broadstone, a handsome neo-classical building on Dublin's North Side, still stands but the Midland Great Western Railway, of which it was the terminus, has long vanished. This meditative poem was written during Fallon's stay in Cornwall and 'the Mount' refers to St Michael's Mount, which he could see from his window.

Page 96 'Athenry'. This very late poem reverts again to the small town in East Galway where the poet was born and where he lived until he left to join the Irish civil service in Dublin, at the age of eighteen.

Founded by the conquering Normans, it was the scene of a famous battle in which the Norman-Irish under de Burgo and de Bermingham defeated and killed the last 'native' Irish King of Connacht, Felim O'Connor. Later, during the rebellion against Elizabeth I, it was taken and sacked by 'Red Hugh' O'Donnell, and later again it suffered under Cromwell. By the poet's time Athenry (*Ath an Rí*, 'the ford of the King') had dwindled to a small farming and market town known mainly for its cattle fairs. In recent years it has honoured its native-born poet with a Padraic Fallon Week and plans to do so again in the near future.

Page 99 'The Small Town of John Coan (2)'. Unlike its predecessor, this sequence appears to be entirely self-contained and relates to no obvious dramatic or narrative context. It was included in a number of poems which Fallon had just completed at the time of his death in October 1974.

Page 107 'A Bit of Brass'. As a boy of eleven, Fallon witnessed the local Irish Volunteers drilling in preparation for their planned uprising in Easter 1916. They even mustered for action on that occasion but, lacking leadership, dispersed anti-climactically to their homes. This was due to the countermanding orders of Eoin McNeill, which virtually confined the rising to Padraic Pearse and James Connolly and their respective followers in Dublin.

Page 110 'The Skellig Way'. The Skelligs are a group of almost sheer rocks – they can hardly be called islands – off the Kerry coast, once the refuge of a community of monks. Their name derives from the word *sceilg*, a rock or cliff.

Page 117 'Dardanelles 1916'. Fallon's memory seems to have led him astray here by a year, since the Dardanelles campaign took place in 1915 and by 1916 most of the surviving British and French troops had been evacuated from the peninsula. The Connaught Rangers – an élite unit which was dissolved some years later – suffered heavily in the campaign, particularly in the fighting around the notorious 'Hill 60' in August 1915, when piled bodies lay rotting in the sun.

Page 119 'Homeric Hymns'. Though Fallon read Latin, he knew no classical Greek and relied mostly on English versions from *The Oxford Book of Greek Verse in Translation*. The fragment of Hesiod is from his *Theogany*.

Page 125 'The Hyperboreans'. From Pindar's Pythian X. The name means 'those who dwell beyond the North Wind' (*Boreas*).

Page 126 'The Infant Heracles'. From Pindar's Nemean I.

Page 128 'Erysichton'. After Hymn 6 of the Alexandrian poet Callimachus. In Greek myth, Erysichton was a man who cut down a grove sacred to Demeter. As punishment, the goddess inflicted him with an insatiable hunger which ruined his whole household.

Page 130 'Solvitur Acris Hiems'. A translation, rather than a free version, of Horace's Ode IV, Book I. It was written partly as a gesture of friendly rivalry towards Louis MacNeice's version, which Fallon admired.

Page 131 'Confessio'. The half-serious, half-bantering confession of the nameless Archpoet is one of the most famous of all medieval Latin poems and has defied various translators, including Helen Waddell in her *Medieval Latin Lyrics*. Scholars have dated it to approximately the year 1169. It was addressed to Reinhold von Dassel, Archbishop-Elect of Cologne and chancellor to the Emperor Frederick I (Barbarossa), and was written in Pavia, the Emperor's base in Northern Italy until his defeat by the Lombard League. As an ancient university town, famous in particular for its law faculty, Pavia was a place of resort for *scholastici vagantes* and also – as is plain from the context – for courtesans. Louis MacNeice's version is much more condensed but does observe the so-called Goliardic metre of seven syllables followed by six.

Page 137 'Two Mallarmé Things for Sue'. Sue (née Lurring) was at this time the wife of Fallon's fifth son, Ivan. She has in her possession slightly different versions of these pieces, given to her personally. I have used the present ones not so much for relative merit, but because they were included in the sheaf of completed poems left by my father at his death.

Page 139 'O Saisons, O Châteaux'. This Rimbaud translation was the very last thing Fallon wrote and was still on his typewriter at the time of his death. At that time he was staying with Ivan and Sue at their home in East Malling, Kent, but in his last illness was taken to hospital in nearby Aylsford, where he died.